MW01628512

To my friend Chris Mitchell
Thank you for your interest
Hope you enjoy our book.

John W. McCahery [illegible]
12 June 2009

LOUIS FROELICH

ARMS-MAKER TO THE CONFEDERACY

JOHN W. MCADEN, JR.

CHRIS E. FONVIELLE, JR.

SlapDash Publishing, LLC
Carolina Beach, North Carolina

LIBRARY OF CONGRESS
CONTROL NUMBER: **2008930192**
John W. McAden, Jr. and Chris E. Fonvielle, Jr.
Louis Froelich - Arms-Maker to the Confederacy
Carolina Beach, N.C., SlapDash Publishing, LLC.
96 pp.

International Standard Book Number
978-0-9792431-4-1

First Printing: **August 2008**

311 Florida Avenue, Carolina Beach, NC 28428
910.232.0604 • info@carolinabeach.net
www.carolinabeach.net

Designed and produced by Daniel Ray Norris (SlapDash Publishing, LLC).
Cover photo by Jack W. Melton, Jr.
Title typefaces: **No. 2 Type, No. 1 Type (The Civil War Press, The Walden Font Company)**
Body typefaces: **Adobe Caslon, Adobe Caslon Pro and Gotham**
Software: **Adobe InDesign CS3, Photoshop, Illustrator and other Adobe products**
Apple Macintosh computers, Xerox printers and Canon imaging products were used in the proofing and production of this book.

IN MEMORY OF

William J. Nicholson III

December 9, 1945 - October 2, 2007

HUSBAND, FATHER, COLLECTOR, FRIEND

The American Society of Arms Collectors, after review by its Publications Committee, has found *Louis Froelich - Arms Maker to the Confederacy* by John W. McAden, Jr. and Chris E. Fonvielle, Jr. to be a useful reference book in the field of Confederate edged weapons.

It is a factual and informative work for both collectors and historians and is recommended for this field of American arms history.

Robert M. Holter, President
J. Craig Nannos, Chair, Publications Committee

July 2008

Contents

Acknowledgements

This project was made possible in large part by the generous assistance of conscientious collectors and preservationists of surviving examples of Louis Froelich's edged weapons and military products. We extend a special thank you to Frederick R. Edmunds, John T. Frawner, Jr., Shannon Pritchard, Tim Terrell, and Clifford M. Young, all of whom went "above and beyond the call of duty" in contributing to *Louis Froelich: Arms-Maker to the Confederacy*. Thanks also to Jack W. Melton, Jr., for his superb photography and Daniel Ray Norris of SlapDash Publishing, LLC for his excellent design and graphics artistry on this project.

With much appreciation, we also recognize the assistance of the following people, businesses, and public institutions.

Gary Albert

American Society of Arms Collectors

Don Barrier

Tom Belton
North Carolina Museum of History, Raleigh

Dan Binder

Peggy Joe Braswell

Cliff Cobb

Robert J. Cooke

Michael DeAngury

Robert DeRosset

Jeff Dickens

Bobby Dixon

Gary Fields

Franklin E. Fussell

Greensboro Museum of History
Greensboro, North Carolina

Halifax County Library, Halifax, North Carolina

Henry Higgins

Betsy Huggins

Donna E. Kelly and Anne Miller
North Carolina Historical Review

Don Koonce

Judy Labbe, James D. Julia, Inc.

Danny Lee

Ben Michel

Bill Moore

Butch Myers

Jo-Anne Nicholson

David Norris

Precision Press, Wilmington, North Carolina
(Nan Pope, Lisa Harrison, Richard Corcoran)

John Sexton

Joseph Sheppard, New Hanover County Public Library
Wilmington, North Carolina

Stephen W. Sylvia, *North South Trader's Civil War*

Don Thorpe

Lewis Leigh, Jr.

Leon H. "Sonny" Sikes

Photography

Jack W. Melton, Jr.
www.jwmelton.com, jack@awmelton.com, 770-633-4446

Daniel Ray Norris - SlapDash Publishing
www.carolinabeach.net, info@carolinabeach.net

Bill Reaves - Images Photography
Wilson, North Carolina

Foreword

Perhaps no other subject holds our interest with such vice-like grip as the War Between the States. More books and articles have been written about this great and tragic conflict than any other in the human experience.

The Civil War has remained front and center in American society, but interest in it is world-wide in scope. It is fascinating, to say the least.

Much attention has been paid by historians and collectors to the advances in weaponry and technology developed and employed during the war. Indeed, there have been many excellent studies on Confederate edged weapons, including those by Richard D. Steuart, William A. Albaugh III, and Fredrick R. Edmunds, to name just a few.

The early publications were invaluable to collectors and enthusiasts interested in Confederate swords, bayonets, knives, and cutlasses, by aiding them in identification and nomenclature. There were errors and misidentifications made early on, but these were largely corrected in subsequent studies.

One of the most recognizable and popular Confederate swords was manufactured by a German immigrant named Louis Froelich. It featured an open brass guard with the letters CSA cast into the knucklebow.

Froelich arrived in the United States shortly before the Civil War began. He was most industrious and inventive, producing a wide variety of swords, knives, buttons, and other products for the Confederacy. Until now, however, the story of his edged weapons' business operations has not been fully examined.

John W. McAden, Jr. and Chris E. Fonvielle, Jr. have provided us with an interesting, well researched, and accurate account of the life and times of Louis Froelich and his genius as an entrepreneurial Confederate industrialist.

Frederick R. Edmunds
Vero Beach, Florida
September 2007

INTRODUCTION

Chris E. Fonvielle, Jr.
Department of History, UNC Wilmington

The Confederacy needed men like Louis Froelich, a North Carolina-based manufacturer of military arms and equipment. Froelich's swords, bayonets, and knives once filled the scabbards of many gray-uniformed soldiers and today are coveted and prized by both private collectors and public museums. His edged weapons have intrigued Civil War enthusiasts for decades, but professional historians have overlooked the important role Froelich played in supplying North Carolina and the Confederacy, largely because so few extant records document his business operations and personal life. The lack of large-scale industrial facilities in the South compelled Richmond and state governments to contract with small, privately owned weapons manufacturing enterprises, including Froelich's Confederate States Armory, to help provide forces with sufficient war materiél. Although quantification of Confederate weapons' production proves difficult, historians believe that such manufacturing establishments provided perhaps as much as one-fourth of the weaponry used by soldiers, sailors, and marines. Louis Froelich's intriguing story sheds light on the issue of Confederate domestic military supply and suppliers.

Military arms collectors generally credit the late William A. Albaugh III as being the first person to identify swords, sabers, and cutlasses manufactured by Louis Froelich, knowledge of which had been forgotten by the twentieth century. Albaugh's discoveries, published in *Confederate Edged Weapons* (1960), have been augmented by the investigations of collectors Frederick R. Edmunds, John T. Frawner, Jr., and John W. McAden, Jr., who revealed their findings on Froelich swords in separate articles in the journal of the American Society of Arms Collectors in the mid-1980s and 1990s. More recently, Cape Fear historian Robert J. Cooke has compiled scarce business and personal information on Froelich, but until now the few studies on Confederate industry and manufacturing by professional scholars—Frank Vandiver's *Ploughshares Into Swords: Josiah Gorgas and Confederate Ordnance*, Richard Goff's *Confederate Supply* and Harold S. Wilson's *Confederate Industry: Manufacturers and Quartermasters in the Civil War*—have omitted any mention of Froelich and other small Confederate industrialists.[1]

Froelich began his career as an arms-maker to the Confederacy in Wilmington, North Carolina, a seaport on the Cape Fear River. How he got to the Tar Heel town, however, is unclear. His trek originated in Bavaria, later a part of Germany, where he was born in 1817. By 1852, Froelich had married Wilhelmina Christine Bissinger, whom family and friends endearingly called Mina. The couple left Bavaria, bound for England, soon after the birth of their first child, Frederick, in January 1853. As they established roots in their adopted country, Mina gave birth in 1854 to a second son, whom they named for his father. Louis senior, meanwhile, found work as a mechanic or machinist with Isambard Kingdom Brunel's renowned engineering and shipbuilding firm in Liverpool.[2]

In 1858, Brunel designed and constructed the great ocean steamship *Leviathan*, renamed *Great Eastern* in 1860, six times larger than any vessel built up to that time. When the *Great Eastern* embarked on her maiden voyage to New York in June 1860, Louis Froelich, accompanied by his family, allegedly was on board. Froelich may have accompanied the ship to make sure her engines performed properly, or perhaps he and his wife had family in the United

States. Whatever Froelich's reason for making the voyage, he arrived in America during the crisis of the Union. One bright spot soon thereafter was the birth of their third son, Charles, while they were staying in New York. By the spring of 1861—perhaps as early as April, but certainly by May—Froelich, along with his wife and their three young boys, were living in Wilmington, North Carolina.[3]

On the eve of the Civil War, Wilmington was North Carolina's busiest seaport and largest city, boasting a population of 9,552 residents, one quarter of whom were foreign-born. A thriving German community of 400 to 500 people comprised the city's largest ethnic minority and may have attracted the Froelich's to the Cape Fear. Or they possibly had family and friends in Wilmington who encouraged them to come south from New York. Whatever the circumstances that led Froelich to Wilmington, he and his family were embraced by the local German people. They quickly settled in, with Mina giving birth to a yet another son, William, in October 1861. Well before then, however, Froelich, who spoke only broken English, had found employment in town as director of a small, newly established button-making firm owned by Jacob Loeb and Lewis Swarzman. The two German-born entrepreneurs were already partners in a grocery, coal, and wood business when they established the Wilmington Button Manufactory in mid-May 1861.[4]

Impressed with their skilled new employee, Loeb and Swarzman announced in the Wilmington *Daily Journal* that the Wilmington Button Manufactory was, as of May 16, "under the direction of Mr. L. Froehlich, a thoroughly educated and scientific mechanic." (The variant spelling Froehlich was common). The Wilmington Button Manufactory produced brass ball buttons (often referred to as Zouave buttons) for military uniforms, and the company advertised

WILMINGTON, N. C., BUTTON MANUFACTORY.

UNDER the direction of Mr. L. FROEHLICH, a thoroughly educated and scientific mechanic, we are enabled to turn out, at the quickest notice, all sizes of UNIFORM BUTTONS.

ALSO—Brass Patterns for Cannon Balls, of every dimension, warranted to be *mathematically correct.*

LOEB & SWARZMAN.

May 16. 213-1m

Louis Froelich first found employment in Wilmington, North Carolina, as director of the newly established Wilmington Button Manufactory, owned by fellow Germans Jacob Loeb and Lewis Swarzman, in mid-May 1861. Froelich's surname was misspelled in this Wilmington newspaper ad announcing his appointment as the head of the button factory.

Wilmington* Daily Journal, *May 16, 1861.

Louis Froelich and his family arrived in Wilmington, North Carolina on the Cape Fear River in the spring of 1861. Wilmington was then the state's largest city and busiest seaport. This woodcut engraving of antebellum Wilmington's waterfront appeared in the July 16, 1853 edition of Gleason's Pictorial Drawing-Room Companion, *a Boston-based illustrated newspaper.*

that it soon hoped to acquire dies for making North Carolina state seal buttons as well. In addition to military uniform buttons, Loeb and Swarzman cast brass patterns for cannonballs "of every dimension, warranted to be *mathematically correct*."[5]

Many sailing vessels and about seventy steamships, including the Lady Sterling, *smuggled vital supplies through the Union naval blockade of Wilmington to help the Confederacy sustain its war effort.*

Courtesy of Chris E. Fonvielle, Jr., Wilmington, North Carolina

Southern forces began organizing, equipping, and training for war months before the attack on Fort Sumter at Charleston, South Carolina, began on April 12, 1861, and military buttons and cannonball patterns, along with hundreds of other items, were desperately needed. Authorities seized more than 150,000 muskets and rifles from U.S. arsenals in the seceded states, but they still faced a shortage of weapons and equipment. That prompted the burgeoning Confederate States of America to turn to the European market, especially Great Britain, for military and civilian goods to aid its war effort. Recognizing that the South would be dependent on Europe for assistance, President Abraham Lincoln declared a naval blockade of the seceded states on April 19, 1861. In a revised proclamation issued eight days later, Lincoln extended the blockade to include North Carolina and Virginia. The small size of the U.S. Navy, the lengthy coastline from Virginia to Texas, and the numerous seaports and harbors to cover, however, prevented the blockade from being effective early on.[6]

A bustling seaport, Wilmington emerged as a popular destination for blockade running ships carrying military arms, equipment, and provisions from overseas. Swift sailing vessels and then steamships began smuggling vital supplies through the Union naval blockade of the Confederate coast, especially rifles, muskets, cannons, swords, bayonets, ammunition, accouterments, cloth and buttons for uniforms, tools, hardware, medicine, blankets, and food, as well as all sorts of civilian goods and luxury items. The USS *Daylight* did not officially place Wilmington under blockade until July 13, 1861. Additional vessels strengthened the blockade over time, capturing or destroying blockade runners more frequently, but blockaders were unable to halt the maritime trade until Wilmington was captured by Union forces in early 1865. By war's end, perhaps 40 percent of all the equipment and supplies used or consumed by Confederate military forces and civilians had entered through the Union blockade.[7]

While blockade running intensified by 1862, the Confederacy also embarked on an ambitious industrial revolution to supplement its European and domestic procurements. Construction of manufacturing facilities, which had been conspicuously neglected in the South before the war, now began in earnest. James B.D. De Bow of Louisiana, Hinton Rowan Helper

of North Carolina, and other critics had warned that a lack of economic diversity, marked by uneven investments in land and slaves, would harm the South's economic health—warnings that now rang true. With only 16 percent of the nation's manufacturing capacity in 1860, the antebellum South was compelled to bring in everything—"from bread, to butter, to baskets," as the saying went—from the North and Europe. After secession, the Confederacy resorted to importing supplies from Europe and, at the same time, building its own industrial base. Otherwise it faced certain and quick defeat.

Although the South lagged far behind the North in industrial capacity, many of its cities, including Wilmington, had enjoyed some manufacturing in

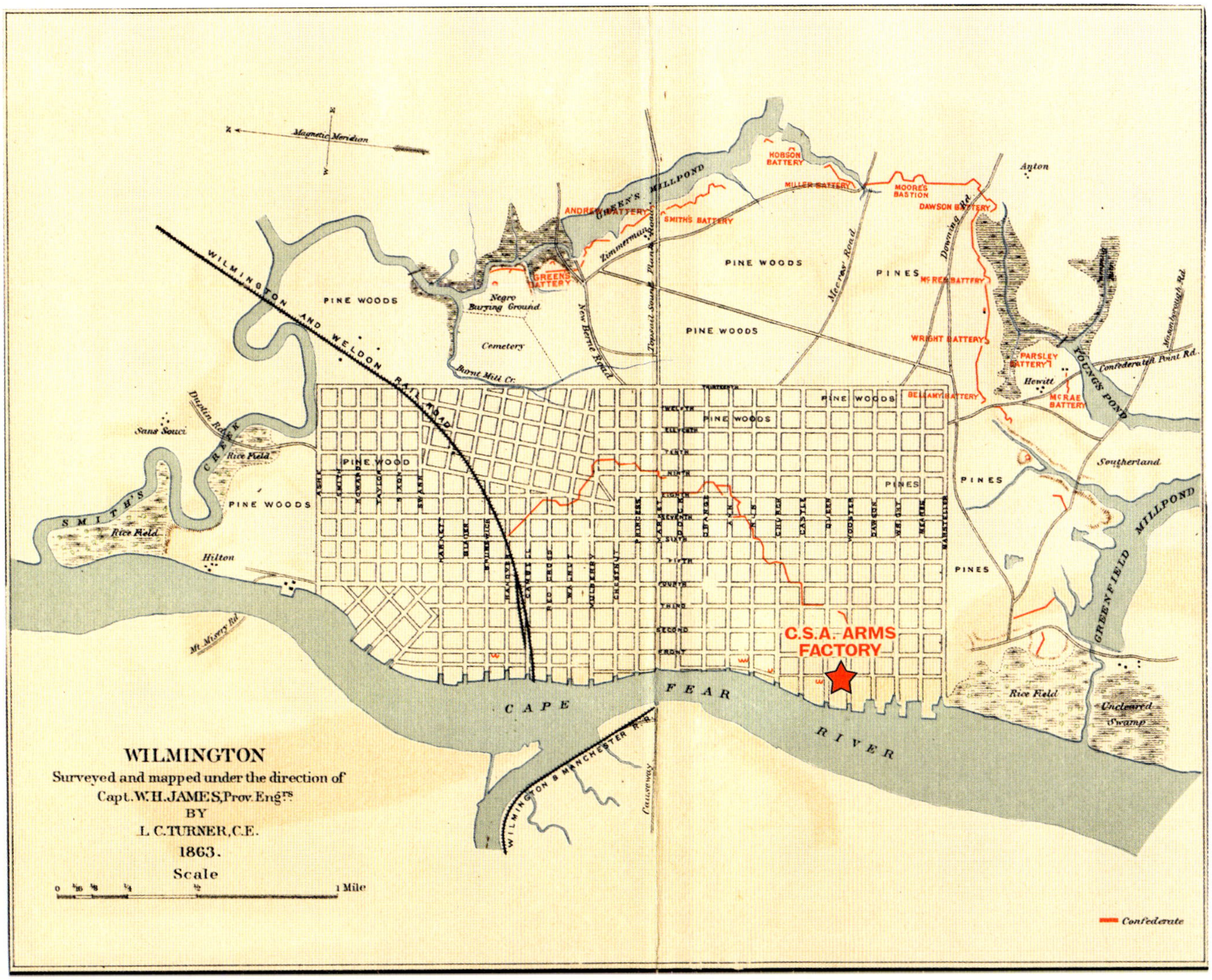

Wilmington, North Carolina, 1863. ***The Official Military Atlas of the Civil War.***

the prewar years. Most manufacturing in the Lower Cape Fear supported the shipbuilding, railroad, and naval stores industries. Antebellum Wilmington boasted two commercial shipbuilding yards—James Cassidey and Son in the city's business district along the Cape Fear River, and Beery's Shipyard on Eagles Island just opposite the city on the river's west bank. During the war, Beery's became known as the Confederate Navy Yard, where a harbor-defending ironclad, the CSS *North Carolina*, was constructed, as well as floating gun batteries and torpedo boats. Clarendon Iron Works and Hart and Bailey Copper and Iron Works manufactured steam engines, portable saw mills, pumps, boilers, water wheels, and an assortment of iron and brass castings. Clarendon Iron Works also repaired railroad locomotives and cars for Wilmington's railroads, as well as ship and boat engines. During the war, the factory also rolled plating for ironclad ships, and fashioned furniture and fittings for gunboats, transports, and blockade runners.[8]

Like Clarendon Iron Works and Hart and Bailey Copper and Iron Works, many Southern manufacturing plants undertook at least some military production to meet the great wartime demand for weapons and equipment. The Tredegar Iron Works in Richmond, Virginia, the largest supplier of artillery and ordnance stores to the Confederacy, served as a model for the establishment of military industrial facilities throughout the South. Under the direction of the Confederate Ordnance Department, former U.S. arsenals in Augusta, Georgia; Charleston, South Carolina; Fayetteville, North Carolina; Little Rock, Arkansas; and Mount Vernon, Alabama, expanded their operations to manufacture additional rifles, ammunition, and gunpowder. Moreover, captured U. S. machinery used in the rifling of muskets, as well as firearms, bayonets, and lances were transported from the battlefront at Harper's Ferry, Virginia, to armories in Richmond and Fayetteville and Asheville, North Carolina. The Fayetteville armory alone produced approximately 8,700 percussion rifles (popularly known as the Fayetteville rifle), patterned after the U.S. Model 1855 longarm, as well as saber bayonets.[9]

Smaller military industrial facilities were soon established in other Southern towns and cities. Contracted by both the Confederate and state governments, these mostly privately-owned and operated factories turned out rifles, muskets, swords, sabers, bayonets, bowie knives, accouterments—cartridge and percussion cap boxes, shoulder and waist belts, and bayonet scabbards—buckles, buttons, boots, shoes, and other articles for military use. About seventy companies manufactured firearms. North Carolina boasted ten known gun factories, not including the state-run arsenal at Fayetteville. Clapp, Gates and Co., Henry C. Lamb and Co., and Mendenhall, Jones and Gardner, all of which were located in Guilford County, produced a total of about 3,000 Model 1841 rifles for North Carolina and the Confederacy. Another thirty identified Southern companies produced swords, bayonets, and bowie knives. Among the more notable businesses were Boyle and Gamble (later Boyle, Gamble and MacFee) and Mitchell and Tyler of Richmond, Virginia, and Kraft, Goldschmidt and Kraft of Columbia, South Carolina. Individual gunsmiths and craftsmen, like sword-makers B. Douglas of Columbia and George Steinmetz of Wilmington, supplemented the efforts of regional factories to keep Southern military forces armed and ready for battle. Some Confederate

manufacturers remain unidentified, known only by surviving examples of their firearms and swords.[10]

The Wilmington Button Manufactory was one such independently owned business established to aid the Southern cause. But the firm, probably like many such small operations, was unable to secure government contracts or failed to sell enough product to make a profit. The Wilmington Button Manufactory closed its doors by the summer of 1861. While Loeb and Swarzman refocused their energies on their grocery and fuel business, Louis Froelich was left unemployed.

A highly skilled craftsman, Froelich did not remain idle for long. Recognizing the great need for arms and equipment in the Confederacy, he soon began producing edged weapons. Froelich was probably one of the local "workmen" who were manufacturing "very serviceable blades. . .both Bowies and Swords," that James Fulton, publisher and editor of the Wilmington *Daily Journal*, examined in mid-July1861. "They were excellent in temper, made of the best steel, and not at all deficient in finish," Fulton observed. "They were, in fact, far superior to the tools made in New England, and with which to sell to the South also."[11]

Fulton's laudable review of the edged weapons then being manufactured in Wilmington impressed W. W. Holden, editor of the North Carolina *Standard* in the state capital of Raleigh. "Sabers, swords and bowie-knives will be greatly needed for the Cavalry and Artillery of this State, and of the Confederate States," Holden responded in his own newspaper. "Our citizens could scarcely do a better service than to get them up as fast as possible. Let them be made so as to be easily wielded and to cut." The *Standard's* correspondent in Wilmington investigated the ensuing industrial production, discovering that, in fact, Froelich was making firearms as well as swords and knives. "Worrell" reported in early August 1861, that "Mr. L. Froelich" had shown him "two handsome horseman pistols" he had crafted, and claimed that he could custom make "rifles, pistols and guns of all kinds." Indeed, Froelich had recently presented a "handsome rifle" of his own design to a North Carolina army officer. "I am sure," Worrell added confidently, "while such men are in Wilmington—men of skill and science—the old North State will never suffer for 'machines' of war."[12]

Machines of war were exactly what Louis Froelich had in mind when, in September 1861, he established a weapons manufacturing firm called the Wilmington Sword Factory, in partnership with a Hungarian immigrant named Bela Estvan. Estvan identified himself as a former cavalry officer in the Hungarian army and a fencing master, and was now, he claimed, a colonel in the Confederate army. He had arrived in Wilmington in June 1861, purportedly to recruit and instruct cavalry in the use of the lance for General Henry A. Wise's legion. The Confederate War Department had commissioned Henry A. Wise, former governor of Virginia, as a brigadier general and authorized him to raise an independent force of volunteer cavalry and infantry. "[Estvan's] standing as a military man and a gentleman is of the highest character," asserted one admirer. Instead of enlisting horse soldiers for General Wise, however, "Colonel" Estvan went into the sword-making business with Louis Froelich. Although the circumstances surrounding their business connection remain unclear, Froelich apparently planned to produce the weapons, while Estvan would handle sales and distribution.[13]

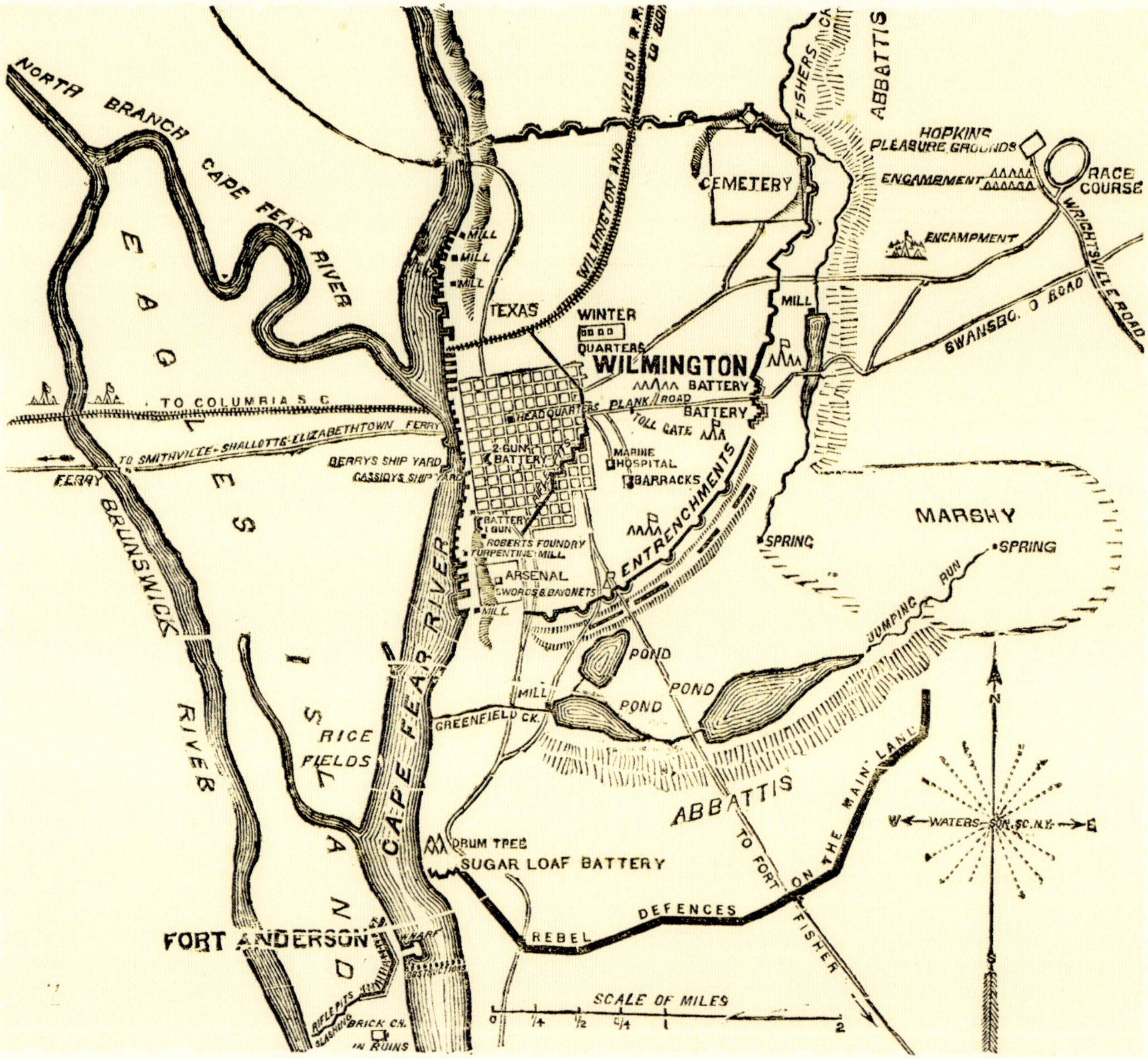

The only extant map of Wilmington during the Civil War that showed the approximate site of Louis Froelich's Confederate States Arms Factory. Located on the southern outskirts of town near the Cape Fear River, Froelich's factory was marked "Arsenal Swords and Bayonets." The fanciful map also showed heavy defensive lines, forts, and batteries protecting the Confederacy's main seaport.

New York Herald, *February 23, 1865*

The Bavarian and Hungarian partners rented space for their factory at Christopher H. Dudley's lumber mill, located below the Clarendon Iron Works on the southern outskirts of Wilmington along the Cape Fear River. As Froelich and Estvan converted Dudley's steam-powered sawmill into a military arms facility, they employed as many skilled craftsmen as they could find—machinists, blacksmiths, strikers, brass molders, brass finishers, polishers, and carpenters —all of whom were paid handsomely for their expertise. "Good reliable" blacksmiths earned the "highest wages," while "good workmen" were paid $3 to $4 a day—four to five times more than an enlisted man made in the Confederate army. Froelich's workers were exempted from military duty so long as they worked in the arms factory.[14]

Many of Froelich and Estvan's employees were German émigrés, including George Grotjohan, Nic Mithler, and George Steinmetz, who was hired as shop foreman until he left in December 1861, to establish a small sword-making business of his own in Wilmington. Edward T. Lucas, a "tinner" (tinsmith) before the war, gave up self-employment in Wilmington to fashion tin hardware—throats and drags for sword and cutlass scabbards—at the Wilmington Sword Factory. Machinist E. Brickhouse and coppersmith Archibald Skipper left Hart and Bailey Copper and Iron Works to work in Froelich and Estvan's factory. Saddlers James Wilson and William Ulrich probably fashioned leather and canvas goods—knapsacks, bowie knife sheaths, bayonet, sword and cutlass scabbards, cartridge boxes,

WANTED IMMEDIATELY,
AT THE WILMINGTON SWORD FACTORY.

5000 LBS. COPPER;
5,000 lbs. Brass,
2,000 lbs. Zinc;
1,000 lbs. Block Tin;
20,000 lbs. German Steel;
10,000 lbs. Spring Steel;
5,000 lbs. Cast Steel;
10,000 Sheets of Sheet Iron, (various sizes);
5,000 Hickory Lance Sticks, 8 feet long, 1⅞ inches, to taper to 1 inch;
5,000 Leather Straps, for Lances;
5,000 Sabre Bayonet Scabbards;
500 Cords Wood, for Steam Engine, for all of which the highest prices will be paid.

ALSO WANTED,

6 Brass Moulders;
30 do. Finishers;
5 Machinists;
20 Polishers.

WANTED,

6 Blacksmiths, and
6 Strikers.

Blacksmiths in town can get contracts for various kinds of work in our line. Please apply early.

☞ The highest wages will be paid for good reliable Blacksmiths at the *Wilmington Sword Factory*. Good workmen will be able to earn from three to four dollars per day

Applications in person, or by letter will be promptly attended. Address

FROELICH & ESTVAN,
Wilmington Sword Factory, Box No. 55, P. O.
Sept. 23d, 1861. 15-2w*

Louis Froelich and his business partner Bela Estvan established the Wilmington Sword Factory in September 1861. They advertised the company's need for both skilled craftsmen and vast quantities of raw material for production.

Wilmington **Daily Journal**, *September 23, 1861.*

percussion cap boxes, belts, and leather- and oilcloth-covered wraps for sword and saber grips. Froelich and Estvan also employed office workers to help them with the day-to-day business of the plant, including Heinrich Westermann, a bookkeeper and militiaman in Wilmington's German Volunteers, and James Barnes, who was employed as a clerk. By October 1861, Froelich and Estvan had also brought on board M. Newhoff, a former Wilmington clothing salesman, as "general agent" in charge of hiring and purchasing. The plant would employ more than seventy men by the late spring of 1862.[15]

In addition to hiring craftsmen to make weapons, Froelich and Estvan advertised that they needed vast quantities of raw materials to begin production. The impressive list included 5,000 pounds of copper, 5,000 pounds of brass, 2,000 pounds of zinc, 1,000 pounds of block tin, 20,000 pounds of German steel, 10,000 pounds of spring steel, 5,000 pounds of cast steel, 10,000 sheets of iron, 5,000 eight-foot long hickory lance sticks, 5,000 leather straps for lances, 5,000 saber bayonet scabbards, 200 bushels of charcoal, and 500 cords of wood to fuel the factory's steam engines. Because such raw materials were scarce and thus highly sought by other manufacturers and the military, Froelich obtained them through public subscription.[16]

Froelich and Estvan retooled Dudley's facilities to manufacture swords, sabers, cutlasses, bayonets, and lances for cavalry. One newspaper reported that the factory also planned to turn out muskets, at which Froelich had already proved capable. The firm also soon began manufacturing weapons under a new name—the C.S.A. Arms Factory (also listed as the Confederate States Arms Factory). The change perhaps reflected the owners' concern that potential customers might mistakenly believe that the Wilmington Sword Factory was limited to the manufacture of only swords. They also wanted the name change to reflect their devotion to the Confederate States of America. The public display of loyalty apparently impressed the government in Richmond and led to a lucrative arms contract.[17]

Despite the new name and steady progress, however, the C.S.A. Arms Factory's output remained low through much of the autumn of 1861. Nevertheless, in early November M. Newhoff informed the Wilmington *Daily Journal* that the plant had received directly from Richmond a "valuable freight car" load of "tools and materials for operating purposes." The tools and equipment would enable the plant to increase production considerably. In the meantime, Newhoff expected the railcar to remain in Wilmington

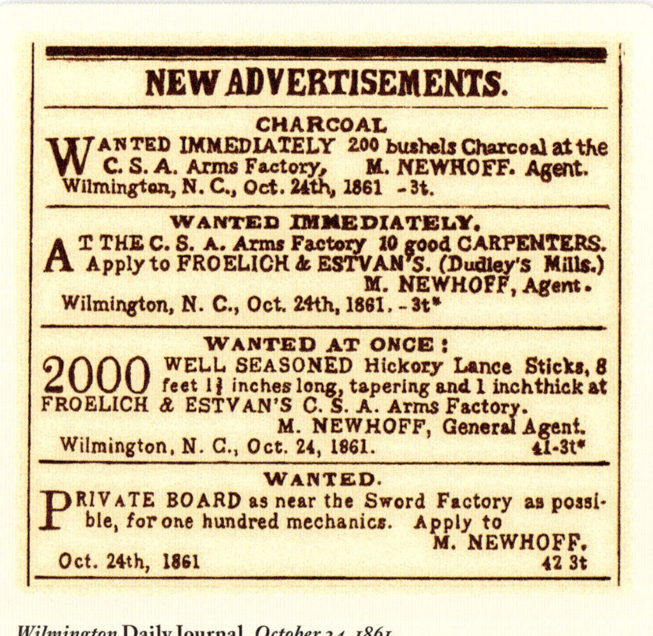

NEW ADVERTISEMENTS.

CHARCOAL

WANTED IMMEDIATELY 200 bushels Charcoal at the C. S. A. Arms Factory, M. NEWHOFF. Agent.
Wilmington, N. C., Oct. 24th, 1861 -3t.

WANTED IMMEDIATELY.

AT THE C. S. A. Arms Factory 10 good CARPENTERS. Apply to FROELICH & ESTVAN'S. (Dudley's Mills.)
M. NEWHOFF, Agent.
Wilmington, N. C., Oct. 24th, 1861. -3t*

WANTED AT ONCE:

2000 WELL SEASONED Hickory Lance Sticks, 8 feet 1½ inches long, tapering and 1 inch thick at FROELICH & ESTVAN'S C. S. A. Arms Factory.
M. NEWHOFF, General Agent.
Wilmington, N. C., Oct. 24, 1861. 41-3t*

WANTED.

PRIVATE BOARD as near the Sword Factory as possible, for one hundred mechanics. Apply to
M. NEWHOFF.
Oct. 24th, 1861 42 3t

Wilmington Daily Journal, *October 24, 1861.*

Confederate vice president Alexander Stephens made an impromptu tour of the Wilmington Sword Factory on the afternoon of November 8, 1861.

Library of Congress, Washington, D.C.

for several days while workmen packed a "load of manufactured implements" to take back to Virginia.[18]

As the C.S.A. Arms Factory geared up to mass-produce edged weapons for the Confederate Ordnance Department, it received some beneficial publicity and praise from a powerful political figure. Confederate vice president Alexander Stephens, unexpectedly delayed as he was passing through Wilmington by rail, accepted an impromptu invitation to tour the arms factory on the afternoon of November 8, 1861. With Estvan absent that day, Froelich and Newhoff, accompanied by civic leaders Judge Joshua G. Wright and Dr. Alexander Medway, led Stephens through the workshops to inspect the machinery and shake hands with workers. They also requested that Stephens help construct the foundation of a "new sword making machine" by laying a brick and spreading on mortar, which he reportedly handled "in a most workmanlike manner." Froelich made the most of the public relations opportunity by presenting the diminutive vice president with a newly manufactured sword and a lance, after which Judge Wright introduced Mr. Stephens to the assembled workmen. Proudly holding his prized possessions amid the applause of the factory men, the vice president made a "spirited address," lauding the industrialists for their energy and patriotism. He urged them to continue their important labor, which he assured them was "no less necessary than that of generals in the field or statesmen in the cabinet." He closed his remarks by thanking them for their warm welcome and generous gifts, which he would take with him "to let other sections see what the Old North State was doing." The local press reported that Stephens was "evidently highly gratified by his visit and reception."[19]

The unexpected appearance of the vice president boosted the morale of the craftsmen at the Wilmington-based arms factory, and they increased their efforts to provide the Confederacy with swords, sabers, bayonets, and accouterments. The earliest Froelich and Estvan voucher for weapons manufactured for the Confederate government, dated November 16, 1861, itemized 128 lances priced at $7.00 each and 220 lance "boots," or leather sheaths to cover the lances' blades, for 72¢ apiece. At the same time, Estvan lobbied to secure a weapons contract from the state of North Carolina. To assist this effort,

Wilmington N.C.
November 30th 1861

His Excellency
Gov H. T. Clark.

Dear Sir

I take pleasure in presenting Mr B. Estvan of the firm of Froelich & Estvan, manufacturers of Arms in this place, who informs me he visits you relative to furnishing you Arms for the State.

I can not recommend too highly these Gentlemen to you. They are largely engaged in the Manufacture of Arms for the Confederate Government, and from what I have seen and know of them, recommend them to your Confidence and Consideration.

Very Truly
Your Obt Servt
Wm Geo. Thomas

William George Thomas, a respected Wilmington doctor and brother-in-law of North Carolina governor Henry T. Clark, wrote a letter of introduction on behalf of Louis Froelich and Bela Estvan.

Governor Henry T. Clark Papers, N.C. State Archives.

William George Thomas, a respected Wilmington physician and brother-in-law of Governor Henry T. Clark, wrote a letter of introduction and recommendation on behalf of Froelich and Estvan. In fact, Estvan carried Dr. Thomas's letter in hand when he visited the state's chief executive in Raleigh in early December 1861. "I take pleasure in presenting Mr. B. Estvan of the firm of Froelich and Estvan, manufacturer of arms in this place, who informs me he visits you relative to furnishing arms for the state," Thomas wrote. "I cannot recommend too highly these gentlemen to you. They are largely engaged in the manufacture of arms for the Confederate government, and from what I have seen and know of them, recommend them to your confidence and consideration."[20]

Governor Clark accepted his brother-in-law's recommendation, awarding Froelich and Estvan a contract to provide edged weapons for North Carolina troops. Soon, the C.S.A. Arms Factory hummed loudly with the sounds of production, as hundreds of bayonets and sabers were turned out each week. On December 13, a load of 232 steel-bladed saber bayonets with brass grips and sheathed in leather scabbards, costing $10.50 per unit for a total of $2,436.00, was invoiced to Captain A.W. Lawrence of North Carolina's Ordnance Department. Following that initial shipment, Froelich and Estvan sent edged weapons by rail to Raleigh on a regular basis during the winter of 1861-1862. For example, 164 bayonets and scabbards were sent on December 28; 17 more on December 31; 90 bayonets on January 4; a large shipment of 220 bayonets on January 6; and 140 more on January 13. After visiting the factory just before Christmas 1861, James Fulton of the Wilmington *Daily Journal* noted that Froelich's artisans were capable of manufacturing 900 cavalry sabers each week, enough to arm a

Half-plate ambrotype of an unidentified cigar-smoking craftsman holding a hammer and a Froelich-manufactured enlisted man's cavalry saber with sword knot and scabbard, and a leather carbine sling over his shoulder.

Courtesy of the William J. Nicholson III estate, Oak Bluffs, Massachusetts.

regiment of horsemen. "We saw the operations of forging the blades—grinding them and polishing them—tempering them and fitting them with handles, involving sundry operations and requiring the services of men of many trades," Fulton reported. "The factory has turned out and is turning out lances, saber bayonets, officers' swords, cavalry sabers, artillery swords and we suppose all other cutting, sticking and stabbing utensils." By late December, the Confederate States Arms Factory was shipping cavalry sabers with buff leather belts and buckles to the state's Ordnance Department at $24.50 each.[21]

SWORDS.

THE great demand for this article has enabled us to make arrangements with a first class Sword Factory to keep us supplied. The Sword will be the same as we have been selling since the commencement of the war, and which has been pronounced by judges to be the best.
Dec. 2. WHITAKER'S Book Store.

Thaddeus Whitaker, proprietor of Whitaker's Book Store in Wilmington, made arrangements probably with the Confederate States Arms Factory to sell its products.

Wilmington **Daily Journal**, *December 2, 1861.*

Wilmingtonians were elated to see the edged weapons factory up and running, as the enterprise meant more jobs and money flowing into the local economy. As one supporter observed: "The inhabitants of Wilmington are indebted for the establishment of these works which will enrich their town by bringing artisans from other places, and a consequent influx of traffic and capital." The factory not only provided work for dozens of men, but merchants profited from the sale of its military products. Whitaker's Book Store at 118 Market Street in Wilmington advertised in the *Daily Journal* that demand for swords among army officers and cavalrymen had prompted them to make "arrangements with a first class Sword Factory to keep them supplied" with blades "pronounced by judges to be the best." Although Whitaker's ad does not explicitly mention the C.S.A. Arms Factory, it appears to suggest a business arrangement with Froelich and Estvan's firm.[22]

Thaddeus Whitaker was in business to sell goods to make money and likely was inexperienced in accurately judging the quality of sabers and bayonets. That job fell to arms inspectors, and examiners in Raleigh were initially unimpressed with some of Froelich's edged weapons being sold to the state of North Carolina. According to Ordnance Department records, the state received 1,474 saber bayonets and 312 cavalry sabers between December 20, 1861, and February 15, 1862. Of those, 54 bayonets and 57 sabers were rejected for being of substandard quality. The C.S.A. Arms Factory probably could have continued to operate with a rejection rate of 3 percent for bayonets, but an 18 percent rejection rate on cavalry sabers was unacceptable. The actual numbers may have been even higher. Governor Clark informed Confederate secretary of war Judah P. Benjamin that three-fourths of the Froelich and Estvan swords the state had purchased proved worthless. Froelich did not want to lose the weapons contract Clark had granted to him only three months earlier. Instead of considering the possibility that he had not yet perfected the art of casting high-quality edged weapons, however, the Bavarian arms-maker suspected that his products were being poorly represented by his business partner. To be sure, something was amiss, prompting Froelich to quickly disassociate himself from the self-proclaimed Hungarian fencing master and cavalry officer.[23]

On the morning of February 24, 1862, Froelich called on Dr. William George Thomas in Wilmington,

expressing concern about his business and his associate, and requesting that Thomas intervene with Governor Clark on his behalf. A sympathetic Thomas wrote again to his brother-in-law, claiming that "[Froelich] has not, somehow, been properly represented either in his partner Mon[sieur] Estvan, or, perhaps, the work which the state has rejected. He can and will do good work; and from what I have seen and know of him, I believe him to be not only a most competent and skillful workman, but an honest man also." The same could not be said, however, of Froelich's estranged collaborator. Thomas informed the governor that Froelich had been "unfortunate in the selection of a partner." What happened exactly to spoil the relationship is not known. The editor of the Richmond *Examiner*, describing Estvan as "an ass and imposter" and "a sleek rascal, smooth spoken and slimy as the serpent in the garden," claimed that the Hungarian cheated Froelich "out of all the funds" and then fled North Carolina. Before going into business with Froelich in Wilmington, Estvan was "previously known in Richmond," where he had opened a military school, "as an unauthorized borrower, and user of other people's money, a thief, a low blackguard, and improvident vagabond." Another detractor, although not as blunt in his assessment, "very much doubted"

GENERAL NOTICES.

NOTICE.

THE public are hereby notified that the partnership heretofore existing between L. Froelich and B Estvan, under the name and style of the "Confederate States Arms Factory," is this day dissolved. The business of the late firm will be continued hereafter by the undersigned.

L. FROELICH.

March 12, 1862. 156-14t

Charleston Courier, Savannah Republican, Richmond Dispatch and Enquirer, Raleigh Standard and State Journal, and Newbern Progress, please copy eight times each and send bill to this office forthwith.

Due to circumstances that are unclear now, Louis Froelich ended his contentious business partnership with Bela Estvan in the Confederate States Arms Factory in March 1862.

Wilmington Daily Journal, *March 12, 1862.*

Estvan's "honesty and fidelity," labeling him a "mere adventurer, a sabrer, a soldier of fortune" and "an unworthy fellow." Having been "found out in his practices," Estvan escaped to New York, only to write a scathing denunciation of the Confederacy in *War Pictures From the South*. The moral of the story, the Wilmington *Daily Journal* claimed, was that "we cannot be too careful—Your mere adventurers. . .are unsafe companions."[24]

WANTED.

10 GOOD BRASS FINISHERS, 4 Saddlers for making acoutrements, Tinsmiths who understand to work Sheetiron, and 2 expert Brass Moulders, at the
C. S. ARMS FACTORY.
May 15th, 1862 210 4t

WANTED.

SHEET BRASS, Scrap Brass and old Copper; also Sheet-iron, at the C. S. ARMS FACTORY.
May 15th, 1862 210 4t

Wilmington **Daily Journal**, *May 15, 1862.*

Froelich officially terminated his partnership with Estvan on March 12, 1862, and, after settling all debts and claims against the Confederate States Arms Factory, determined to continue the military arms business in Wilmington on his own. Throughout the spring and summer of 1862, Froelich produced hundreds of saber bayonets, cavalry sabers, staff and field swords, lances, artillery short swords, naval cutlasses, cartridge and percussion cap boxes, belts, knapsacks, and copper North Carolina sunburst buttons for military uniforms. State Ordnance Department records reveal that between early March and September 1862, he sold to the state 855 saber bayonets; 565 cavalry sabers; 129 staff and field swords and belts; 318 artillery short swords; 216 lances (16 with bridle cutters); 4 vices; and one "F&S musket" (perhaps a Froelich prototype). The quality of Froelich's work proved satisfactory as few blades were rejected by the state's quality control inspectors. Froelich also reportedly manufactured a new "efficient weapon"—a "thirty-six shooter Rifled Revolver," capable of firing bullets up to 1,400 yards. The swivel gun was mounted on a horse-drawn wagon protected by a triangular-shaped bullet-proof shield made of iron and loop-holed for firing. "[It] will be well adapted to out-post

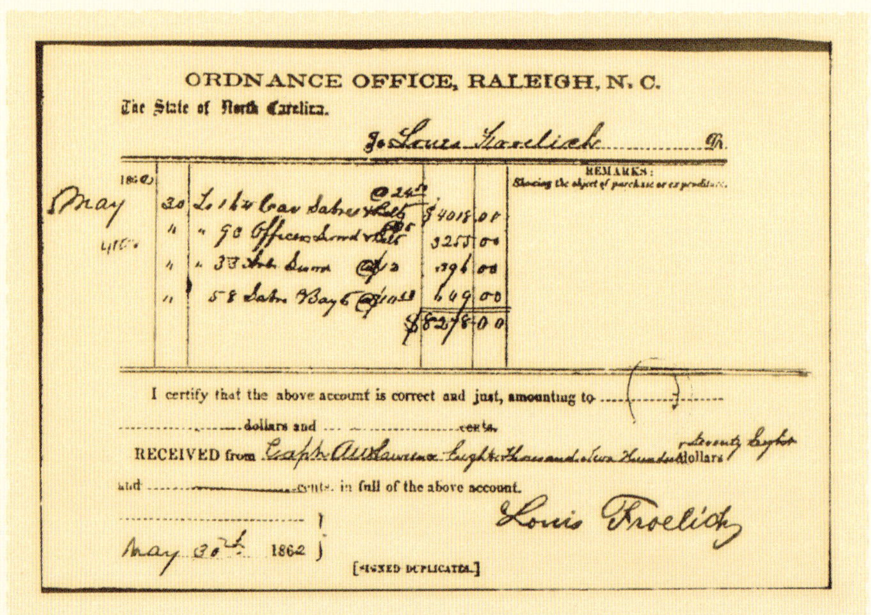
ORDNANCE OFFICE, RALEIGH, N. C.

The State of North Carolina.

To Louis Froelich Dr.

REMARKS: Showing the object of purchase or expenditure.

1862 May 30 — $4018 00; $3255 00; $396 00; $609 00; $8278 00

I certify that the above account is correct and just, amounting to ... dollars and ... cents.

RECEIVED from Capt. A W Lawrence ... Dollars and ... cents, in full of the above account.

Louis Froelich

May 30th 1862

[SIGNED DUPLICATES.]

Rare extant receipt written to Captain A.W. Lawrence for Froelich cavalry sabers and belts, officers' swords and belts, artillery short swords, and saber bayonets sold to the North Carolina Ordnance Department, May 30, 1862.

National Archives, Washington, D.C.

or picket duty, from its long range, accuracy of fire, number of shots and protection of gunner," one admirer proclaimed. Although Froelich constructed a prototype "Rifled Revolver," he did not mass-produce the weapon, as no examples have been identified.[25]

Colonel Robert H. Cowan, commander of the 18th Regiment North Carolina Troops, received a "fine sword and belt" as a gift from Louis Froelich shortly after the battle of Slash Church, Virginia.

Courtesy of Robert DeRosset, Charlotte, North Carolina.

While Froelich worked hard to restore his credibility as a master arms-maker with both the Confederate and North Carolina ordnance departments, he also launched a public relations campaign to improve his company's reputation with rank-and-file soldiers, who were some of his best customers. In early June 1862, he and his employees donated $328.25 to soldiers of the 18th Regiment North Carolina Troops who had been wounded in the battle of Slash Church, Virginia, on May 27. All of the regiment's companies came from southeastern North Carolina, and three of them had been organized in Wilmington—Company A (German Volunteers), Company G (Wilmington Light Infantry), and Company I (Wilmington Rifle Guards). Froelich personally knew soldiers in the German Volunteers, entry into which required German heritage, and some of whom he would employ when they returned home from the war. Froelich also donated a "fine sword and belt" to the 18th North Carolina's commanding officer, Colonel Robert H. Cowan of Wilmington. In appreciation, Cowan addressed an open letter, published in the June 23, 1862 edition of the Wilmington *Daily Journal*, to the "generous and patriotic men" of the Confederate

States Arms Factory. "On behalf of the regiment," the colonel wrote, "I beg that you will return to the gentlemen of the Factory our very sincere thanks. . . and although they are not in the field, are doing no less service to our cause." Cowan went on to extend his personal thanks to Louis Froelich for "his handsome present," promising to keep the sword drawn until the South had won its independence. "It shall never be sheathed, with my consent," he declared, "until the 'Confederate States of America' are acknowledged among the nations of the earth."[26]

WANTED IMMEDIATELY.
10 BLACKSMITHS to forge Sword Blades. As the same go on piece work, they can make from 5 to 10 dollars per day.
Also, Blacksmiths who want to take contracts for forging, will please call at L. FROELICH.
Confederate States Armory,
Wilmington, N. C.
Aug. 15th, 1862 287-6t

Wilmington Daily Journal, *August 15, 1862.*

Froelich's professional integrity was well on its way to being restored, and he bolstered arms production at the newly renamed Confederate States Armory in the summer of 1862. An unexpected natural catastrophe, however, abruptly interrupted operations at the factory when a yellow fever epidemic struck Wilmington in September. Wilmingtonians believed that the blockade runner *Kate* had inadvertently smuggled the pestilence into the city along with her cargo of military supplies when she docked on August 6, 1862. Ironically, the first confirmed yellow fever victim was Lewis Swarzman, Froelich's former employer with the Wilmington Button Manufactory, who died on September 9, 1862. Unfamiliar with the virus and its mosquito-borne transmission, Wilmington's physicians misdiagnosed the disease until it reached epidemic proportions in late September. As cases and fatalities mounted, citizens evacuated the town for places of refuge in the interior of the state or closer to the ocean. Wilmington became a virtual ghost town as homes and businesses were closed and boarded up, and streets stood empty and silent except for the sounds of caregivers treading the walkways and death wagons rolling toward the cemeteries.[27]

Louis Froelich was concerned about the health of his employees and, like most Wilmington businessmen, reluctantly gave in to the prevailing fear of fever. On his instructions, work stopped at the Confederate States Armory on September 27, with "all employees discharged until the health of town has improved." In fact, production had slowed to a trickle weeks earlier as Froelich shipped no weapons to Raleigh after August 15, and only four vises by September 3, 1862. Perhaps Froelich had no choice but to halt operations as his workers fled the city. The factory's bookkeeper, Heinrich Westermann, courageously remained behind to receive contracts and buy materials, but even Froelich and his family evacuated, seeking refuge in Kenansville, a small town in Duplin County, North Carolina, sixty miles north of Wilmington. Captivated by Kenansville, Froelich purchased land soon after his arrival there, buying 2 ½ acres of property from Alsa Sutherland on September 30, 1862. Froelich must have considered the possibility that, with yellow fever ravaging Wilmington, he might have to relocate his factory to fulfill his business obligations.[28]

Having escaped the plague in Wilmington, Froelich and most of his employees survived the dreaded disease, but not all of them. Froelich's trusted agent M. Newhoff succumbed to the fever even though he,

CONFEDERATE STATES ARMORY
WILMINGTON, N. C., Sept. 27, 1862.

THIS ARMORY will stop work from this day, on account of the prevailing fever. All employees are herewith discharged until the health of the town has improved, when the recommencement of work of the Armory will be duly advertised.

Mr. H. Westermann, who will transact my business in my absence, will receive contracts for arms, buy up materials, etc., as usual. L. FROELICH.

Sept. 27th, 1862.—18-1w

In early August 1862, the dreaded yellow fever virus was inadvertently imported into Wilmington on board the blockade runner Kate. *When an epidemic gripped the city by the following month, Louis Froelich halted production at the Confederate States Armory and departed the city along with thousands of other residents.*

Wilmington* Daily Journal, *September 27, 1862.

too, had departed the city. Newhoff was undoubtedly infected before he left the coast. He made it as far as Fayetteville, North Carolina, eighty-two miles up the Cape Fear River from Wilmington, before the virus overcame him. He was immediately placed in quarantine, but died on September 30, 1862, the same day Froelich was buying land in nearby Kenansville. Froelich workers Andrew Craig, who passed away on September 21, and Thomas C. Capps, who died seven weeks later on November 10, 1862, in Wilmington, may also have been casualties of the epidemic. In Wilmington alone at least 654 citizens went to their graves as a result of the yellow fever before cold weather killed the disease.[29]

As the epidemic waned in the late autumn of 1862, Froelich was among those who slowly returned to Wilmington. He recommenced operations at the armory by late November, instructing blacksmiths to report to work on the 20th and metal finishers one week later. Along with weapons manufacturing, Froelich resumed production of accouterments and other equipment. On November 26, he invoiced the Confederate Ordnance Department for ninety-nine saber belts at $3.00 apiece and another thirty-four saber belts at $4.00 each. Froelich's accouterments apparently were in high demand, as he advertised in the Wilmington *Daily Journal* on December 17, 1862, that he was looking to hire "25 steady and able workmen to go on Leather Work and Knapsacks." The factory's shutdown for almost two months, however, had placed a financial burden on the plant's operations and employees, and it was going to take some doing to get weapons and accouterments steadily rolling out and money rolling in again. North

CONFEDERATE STATES ARMORY,
WILMINGTON, N. C., Nov. 20th, 1862

THIS ARMORY will commence to work again from this date. All Blacksmiths having been in our employ are wanted immediately. Finishers will commence on Thursday the 27th of this month. L. FROELICH.

Nov. 20. 35 3t

Fayetteville Observer, Raleigh Standard and Richmond Enquirer copy three days, and send bills to this office.

Wilmington Daily Journal, *November 20, 1862.*

Carolina's Ordnance Department records indicate that Confederate States Armory saber bayonets were not received again in Raleigh until February 28, 1863.[30]

By January 1863, however, the Wilmington armory was probably fully operational again. To promote the weapons they were making and to display their patriotism, workmen from the factory organized themselves into a militia company, electing William M. Lewis as captain, Englehard Schulken as first lieutenant, G. T. Moore as second lieutenant, and Kenneth McKenzie as first sergeant. Not even a small fire that burned a detached dwelling and tin house at the plant on January 10 dampened the enthusiasm of the proud home guardsmen. The militiamen, bearing Froelich-manufactured lances adorned with colorful pennants, their newly elected officers at the head of the column, turned out in public on Saturday, January 17, 1863.[31]

CONFEDERATE STATES ARMORY,
WILMINGTON, N. C., Dec. 17, 1862.

WANTED—25 steady and able workmen, to go on Leather Work and Knapsacks.
Also, 5 or 6 good Blacksmiths, to go on Piece Work.
L. FROELICH.

Dec. 17, 1862. 58-6t

When the yellow fever epidemic in Wilmington finally ended in the late autumn of 1862, Louis Froelich recommenced operations at the Confederate States Armory, advertising for skilled craftsmen to join his workforce.

Wilmington Daily Journal, *December 17, 1862.*

Public display, however, soon turned to private disaster when fire swept through the Confederate States Armory during the early morning hours of February 20, 1863. The alarm went out about 3:00 a. m., but the fire brigade could not save the industrial complex. The huge blaze of unknown origin destroyed all hopes of Froelich rebuilding at the Dudley site along the Cape Fear River, and he was compelled to move his military arms business elsewhere. On March 12, 1863, exactly

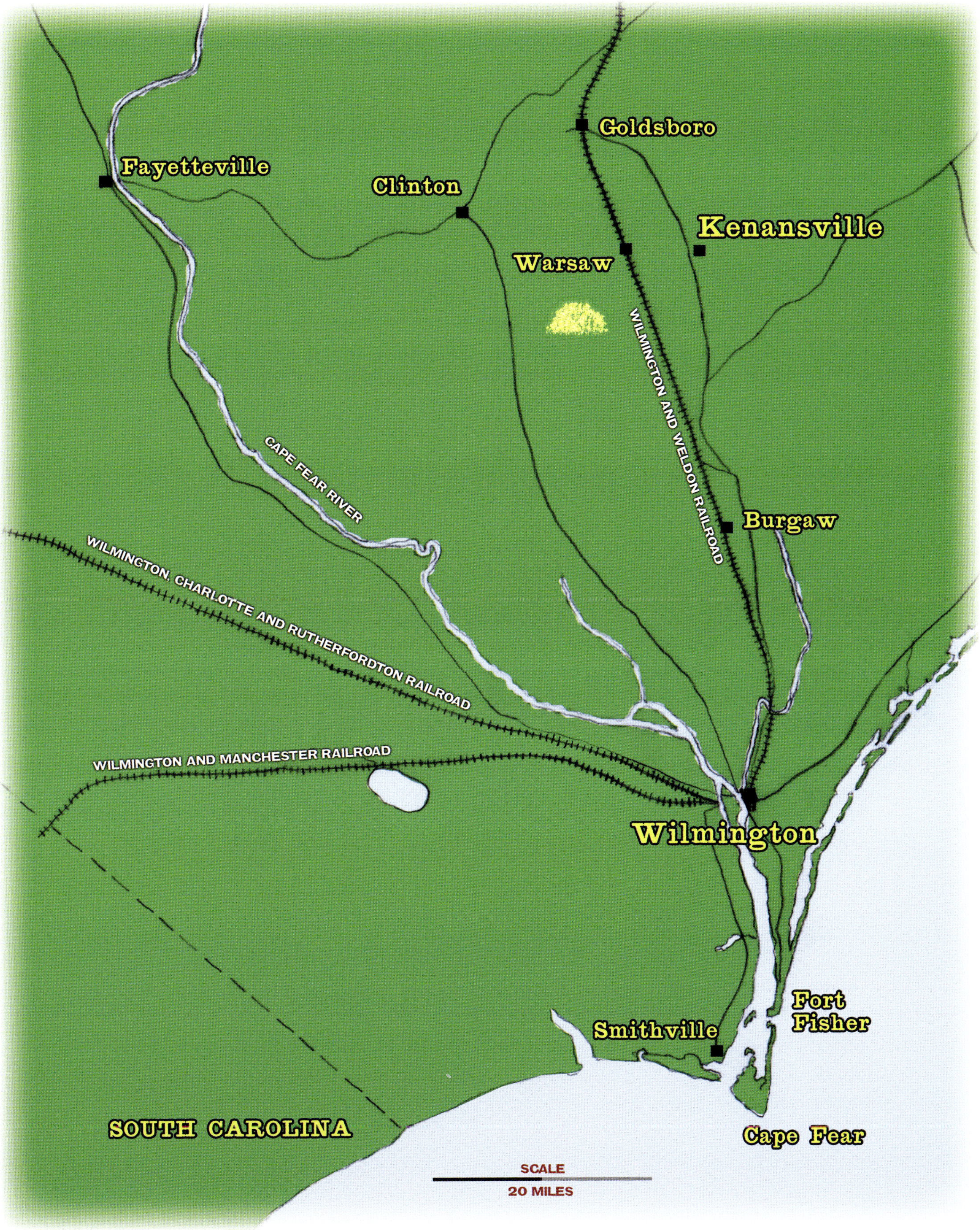

Goldsboro
Fayetteville
Clinton
Kenansville
Warsaw
WILMINGTON AND WELDON RAILROAD
CAPE FEAR RIVER
Burgaw
WILMINGTON, CHARLOTTE AND RUTHERFORDTON RAILROAD
WILMINGTON AND MANCHESTER RAILROAD
Wilmington
Fort Fisher
Smithville
SOUTH CAROLINA
Cape Fear
SCALE
20 MILES

CONFEDERATE STATES ARMORY,
WILMINGTON N. C., March 12th, 1863.
THIS ARMORY is removed to Kenansville N. C. All orders, letters, etc., must be directed to that place.
L. FROELICH.
March 12, 1863. 130-1w

A destructive fire at the Confederate States Armory in Wilmington on February 20, 1863, compelled Louis Froelich to relocate his factory to Kenansville, North Carolina, the following month.

Wilmington Daily Journal, *March 12, 1863.*

one year to the day after he dissolved his partnership with Bela Estvan, Froelich publicly announced in the Wilmington *Daily Journal* that his armory had relocated to Kenansville, North Carolina. The new factory site was situated on the west side of town at the intersection of the Wilmington and Warsaw roads and not too distant from the Wilmington and Weldon Railroad, providing direct rail links to important junctions from the Carolina coast to Virginia, including Wilmington, Warsaw, Goldsboro, and Weldon in North Carolina, and Petersburg in southeastern Virginia.[32]

Froelich notified his employees in Wilmington that they should report to work "without delay" at the Confederate States Armory, or else, if they were liable, face conscription. Most craftsmen apparently moved to Kenansville, for by March 24, 1863, Froelich reported that his factory was "again in full operation." On April 29, he contracted to furnish 500 sets of infantry accouterments at $13.00 per set to the Confederate Quartermaster Department in Richmond, guaranteeing delivery of 150 sets by June 1 and 50 sets per week over the following seven weeks. He inked another deal on September 16, 1863, to provide an additional 120 sets of accouterments. Contracts and profits must have been coming in as Froelich bought more land in Duplin County, presumably to expand his operations.[33]

Froelich maintained close ties to Wilmington even after his relocation to Kenansville, the place with which he is most closely associated as arms-maker to the Confederacy. He enjoyed a large customer base among military personnel in Wilmington, and

C. S. ARMORY.
KENANSVILLE, March 24, 1863.
THIS ARMORY is again in full operation. All absent employees are hereby given notice to report without delay at this place, to go to work. Those that do not report by the 1st of April, will be ordered, if liable to conscription, to the Camp of Instruction at Raleigh, as per order from Head Quarters, Raleigh. L. FROELICH.
March 24, 1863. 140 6t*.

Wilmington Daily Journal, *March 24, 1863.*

was more likely to obtain much needed domestic or blockade-run manufacturing materials there than in the Carolina countryside. To represent his interests at the seaport, Froelich hired German-born Claus Tienken as purchasing agent, and appointed James McCormick as contract agent. McCormick ran a dry goods store on Market Street in Wilmington, where he carried a "fine assortment" of Froelich swords, belts, and other military equipment, and now would also accept orders for the same.[34]

SWORDS, BELTS AND MILITARY EQUIPMENTS

MR. JAMES McCORMICK has been appointed agent in Wilmington, for the Confederate States Armory, and will take orders for Swords, Belts and Military Equipments generally.

Mr. McCormick has now on hand at his Store on Market Street, a fine assortment of the above articles manufactured at the Armory, which he will take pleasure in showing to all parties desirous of purchasing.

M. FROELICH,
Proprietor Confederate States Armory.

May 6, 1863. 176-6t.

Louis Froelich appointed James McCormick to make sales and take orders in Wilmington for the Confederate States Armory, now based in Kenansville, North Carolina.

Wilmington* Daily Journal, *May 6, 1863.

Froelich worked hard to establish his new armory at Kenansville, but misfortune soon struck again. Flames once more destroyed the factory, as they had in Wilmington. This time, however, there was no question as to the source of the fire—it was intentionally set by Union soldiers.

By the spring of 1862, United States Army and Navy forces had captured and occupied most of North Carolina's coastal plain, from Albemarle Sound to White Oak River, only sixty miles up the coast from Wilmington. To disrupt Confederate lines of communication and transportation, the Union army

NOTICE.

I WISH TO PURCHASE for Confederate States Armory, at Kenansville, N. C.,

COPPER,
ZINK,
BLOCK TIN,
SHEET IRON,
BRASS.

Also, 100,000 lbs. of MOSS.

Any one wishing to contract for the same will please make application to CLAUS TINKENS,
At Wilmington.

Nov. 18. 60-14t.

Claus Tienken, whose surname was misspelled in this newspaper ad, served as purchasing agent in Wilmington for the Confederate States Armory as of November 18, 1863.

Wilmington* Daily Journal, *November 18, 1863.

occasionally advanced inland to attack strategic targets, especially the Wilmington and Weldon Railroad, a major supply line for General Robert E. Lee's Army of Northern Virginia. The rail line at Warsaw was the target when, on July 3, 1863, Major General John G. Foster, commander of Union army forces in North Carolina, dispatched Lieutenant Colonel George W. Lewis with 650 horsemen of the 3rd New York Cavalry, two companies of the 23rd Battalion New York Cavalry, and Company L, 1st North Carolina Union Volunteers from their base at New Bern on Pamlico Sound.

The westward route to Warsaw took Lewis's rapidly moving mounted column toward Kenansville, where a vanguard detachment under Major Ferris Jacobs, 3rd New York Cavalry, arrived on the afternoon of July 4, surprising the townspeople and a company of Confederate cavalry stationed in the area. The Federals quickly dispersed the gray-clad horsemen and secured the town. Lieutenant Colonel Lewis and the main force came up about one o'clock the following morning, and proceeded to torch Froelich's factory, or, as Lewis described it, "an armory and saddle manufactory." There is no evidence that Froelich's employees had organized themselves into a militia company in Kenansville as they had in Wilmington, or offered any resistance to the raiders as they swarmed onto the factory grounds.

After completing their mission at Kenansville, the Federals moved on to Warsaw, where they damaged railroad tracks for three or four miles up and down the Wilmington and Weldon line. By the time the raiding party returned to New Bern on July 8, Lieutenant Colonel Lewis estimated that it had ridden 170 miles and ruined "nearly a million dollars worth of property," much of it at the Confederate States Armory. In burning the factory, the officer reported, the Federals had destroyed a "large quantity of sabers, saber bayonets, knives, and all kinds of arms of that description," as well as tools, saddles, and a commissary storehouse loaded with food. After hearing Lewis's account of the raid, General Foster informed his superiors in Washington that the cavalry force had destroyed "some 2,500 sabers and large quantities of saber bayonets, bowie knives, and other small-arms" at the Kenansville armory.[35]

To what extent Froelich recovered from the devastation to his new plant is unclear. He did rebuild the business at Kenansville and continued to manufacture arms and equipment for the Confederacy, as evidenced in part by an advertisement placed in the November 21, 1863, edition of the Wilmington *Daily Journal*, which announced that the Confederate States Armory was looking to purchase copper, zinc, block tin, and sheet iron for production, and 100,000 pounds of moss, probably for use as packing material. Moreover, invoices to the Confederate Ordnance Department reveal that Froelich delivered 200 knapsacks to Richmond by January 4, 1864, and 23 swords, 436 sabers, and 133 saber bayonets by January 25, 1864. Froelich was hard pressed for investment capital as a result of the loss of his second factory, however, and took on a new business partner, Jacob H.N. Cornehlson, in early January 1864.[36]

Cornehlson, a native of Hanover, Germany, had immigrated with his family to Wilmington before the war and worked as a barkeeper at Sharpsteen and Cornehlson, a saloon, billiards hall, and bowling alley co-owned by James P. Sharpsteen and Christian Cornehlson, Jacob's brother. Besides working together, the Cornehlson brothers were also members of the German Volunteers, which became Company A, 18th Regiment North Carolina Troops during the war. Both of them served as privates in the Confederate army for one year, but returned to Wilmington after their terms of enlistment had expired in April 1862. The Cornehlsons continued to run the saloon and billiards hall even after Jacob bought half interest in the Confederate States Armory on January 1, 1864. Froelich acknowledged payment of $29,930.62 on February 25, and an article of agreement was recorded at the Duplin County registrar of deeds' office on March 1, 1864. The business was officially listed as Louis Froelich and Company.[37]

Beyond Froelich's association with Jacob Cornehlson, little is known about the Confederate States Armory for the remainder of the war. An article titled "Home Industry" in the April 28, 1864, edition of the Wilmington [Weekly] *Journal*, reported that between April 1, 1861 and March 1, 1864, "Messrs. L. Froelich & Co. of Kenansville, N.C. manufactured 18 sets of surgical instruments, 800 gross of military

buttons, 3,700 lance spears, 6,500 saber bayonets, 11,700 cavalry sabers, 2,700 officer's sabers, 600 navy cutlasses, 800 artillery cutlasses, 1,700 sets of infantry accouterments, 300 saber belts, and 300 knapsacks." Yet Froelich continued producing military arms and equipment after March 1864. The Confederate Ordnance Department received 645 sabers, now priced at $28.00 each, and 293 knapsacks for $6.00 apiece, by May 2, 1864, and an additional 97 sabers four days later.[38]

Ambrotype of an unidentified Confederate officer holding a Froelich-made enlisted man's cavalry saber.

Courtesy of John W. McAden, Jr.

Two extant pieces of correspondence and a few additional invoices cast only the dimmest light on Froelich's operations in Kenansville late in the war. In a letter dated June 7, 1864, to Captain James Dinwiddie of the Confederate Ordnance Department, Froelich responded to instructions from Richmond to discontinue the manufacture of knapsacks, and a memo from Captain Dinwiddie to Froelich, dated November 9, 1864, concerned payment of a contract. The last known shipments of Froelich products to the Confederacy comprised thirty pounds of candles on November 12, one sword and belt on November 24, and thirty axes on December 31, 1864. In all likelihood, the Confederate States Armory continued to manufacture weapons, accouterments, and a variety of supplies and hardware for both North Carolina and the Confederacy until the Union army occupied southeastern North Carolina by March 1865.[39]

Louis Froelich and his family lived in Kenansville for at least five years after the war. As late as September 1869, Froelich was still buying property

L. FROELICH, & Co
Proprietor

Confederate States Armory,

Kenansville, N. C., [illegible] 7th, 1864

Capt. Jas. Dinwiddie
Ordnance Dept.
Richmond Va
Sir

Yours of the first inst. recd. In reply I would respectfully inform you that I recd. about the beginning of Feby. last an order from Col. Brown through Maj. Taylor to discontinue the manufacture of knapsacks. What I had then on hand have been delivered

Yours very Respectfully
Louis Froelich

In a letter on scarce Confederate States Armory letterhead, Louis Froelich responded to Captain James Dinwiddie of the Confederate Ordnance Department concerning instructions to discontinue the manufacture of knapsacks.

National Archives, Washington, D.C.

in Duplin County where he owned almost twenty-six acres of land at one time or another. By 1866, however, Froelich was no longer using his land for manufacturing weapons of war, but for planting fruit trees, grapevines, and flowers. He had turned his swords into plowshares to become one of North Carolina's leading horticulturalists, possessing as much expertise in that endeavor as in weapons manufacturing.[40]

Froelich's sons Frederick and Louis became farmers like their father. In the spring of 1866, young Frederick, then only thirteen years old, and his eleven year old brother Louis, planted 200 apple trees, seventy-five peach trees, forty pear trees, fifteen plum trees, six apricot trees, ten fig trees, one English walnut tree, twenty-one scuppernong grape vines, and 350 assorted grape vines, all under the supervision of their father. The Froelich boys were determined to help rebuild the devastated South in the postwar years, one tree and one farm at a time, and they implored other young men to follow their example. "This is no time for playing, but we must clear away the ruins from our fathers' homes, and build up new foundations," Frederick wrote. "We must work for our fathers and brothers slain on the battle fields, and we must work for our fathers and mothers who have been deprived of all comforts." Then, drawing on the good works from the good hands of the nation's founding father, Frederick reminded Southerners to "keep the noble words of George

Washington before your eye: 'Agriculture is the most healthful, and the most noble employment of man.'" The Froelichs profited handsomely from their hard work in the fields. Frederick claimed that the family cleared a profit of $2,663.25 from their agricultural pursuits in 1870. [41]

In August 1870, the Froelichs exhibited numerous varieties of their grapes, apples, pears, peaches, fruit preserves, vegetables, flowers, and both domestic and foreign wines at the first annual Cape Fear Horticultural Fair in Wilmington. The Cape Fear Agricultural Association had been formed the previous year to promote agriculture, commerce, and mechanical arts in Wilmington and the surrounding area. The Wilmington *Morning Star* reported that "Mr. Louis Froelich of Kenansville, Duplin County, who is noted for his deep interest he has always taken in matters pertaining to the Agricultural and Horticultural interests in this section, and of the State at large, was well represented in the different departments." Froleich was awarded first prize certificates for the largest variety of pears, and the best tomato jelly and still wines. He was also given a diploma for the second largest variety of table apples, while Mrs. Froelich took home a "Fancy Work and Millinery" certificate for best beadwork. Froelich was especially proud of his large, sweet "Improved Scuppernong Grape," of which he had grown 100 bushels that season and from which he had produced several delectable wines, including a "Sparkling Burgunda." For Louis Froelich, swords and sabers had given way to scuppernong grapes, and he established himself in effect the father of the now thriving Duplin County wine industry. And he was quite philosophical about wine production. "Good wine makes good blood, good blood causes good humor, and good humor causes good thoughts, and good thoughts bring forth good works, and good works carry a man to Heaven," Froelich opined.[42]

Sometime after 1870, Froelich relocated his family to a farm near Enfield in Halifax County, North Carolina. He may have moved there to be closer to vineyards owned by C.W. Garrett and Company, where he grew some of his popular grapes, or to distance himself from creditors. Froelich had already transferred ownership of his Kenansville home to his wife, Wilhelmnia, and given power of attorney to his brother-in-law, Charles F. Bissinger. One of his creditors was the Wilmington grocery business of Alexander Adrian and Hanke Vollers and he apparently lost property to debt payment. Froelich evidently had a bad turn of financial fortune, perhaps due to a chronic illness. As early as the spring of 1866, Frederick Froelich observed that his father was "more or less sick."[43]

Halifax County turned out to be Louis Froelich's last place of residence. There he died of consumption (tuberculosis) on October 27, 1873, at the age of fifty-six. "Mr. Louis Froelich, formerly a resident [of Wilmington]...did much in the way of developing the resources of this section and was an active contributor to the success of the Agricultural Fairs in this city. He paid particular attention to the grape culture, in which he was very successful, his wines being always among the best exhibited at the various fairs," noted the Wilmington *Morning Star*. "His many friends will regret to hear of his death, as he was among the most useful men of his day and generation." The obituary made no mention of Froelich's career as a military arms-maker to North Carolina and the Confederacy.[44]

All remnants of the Wilmington Sword Factory and the Confederate States Armory at Kenansville are gone. Historians have pinpointed the general area of the Wilmington armory, but the site remains unexcavated by archaeologists. The location of the Kenansville armory has never been lost to public memory. In 1949, the North Carolina Highway Historical Marker commission erected a marker commemorating the "Confederate Arms Factory." Commercial development in recent years has covered much of the plant site, but a Civil War Trails marker was erected on the historic grounds in October 2004. An updated Highway Historical Marker, now recognizing the "Confederate Armory," was installed in 2007.

This small grove of trees may mark Louis Froelich's burial site on the "Froelich Farm" near Enfield in Halifax County, North Carolina.
Courtesy of John W. McAden, Jr.

Louis Froelich's final resting place, however, has been lost. Presumably he was buried on his Halifax County property, which is still known as the "Froelich farm" in that part of North Carolina. After her husband's untimely death, Mrs. Froelich moved to the nearby town of Halifax, where she apparently spent the remainder of her life. Mina, who was thirteen years younger than Louis, outlived him by more than thirty-one years. She passed away on January 8, 1905, and was buried in a small family plot in Halifax.

The North Carolina Highway Historical Marker commission replaced an old 1949 marker with this updated marker in 2007 to commemorate the Confederate States Armory in Kenansville, North Carolina.

Courtesy of Franklin E. Fussell, Kenansville, North Carolina.

Louis Froelich's edged weapons and his legacy as a master arms-maker to the Confederacy, however, have survived. The Bavarian craftsman immigrated to America seeking a new life, only to find himself situated in the South when the Civil War began. Froelich took advantage of the opportunity to provide for his growing family by manufacturing much-needed weapons and equipment for North Carolina and Confederate troops. His skills as an industrial craftsman are evident in examples of his now scarce swords, sabers, bayonets, bowie knives, and lances. "The edged weapons made by Froelich after his episode as Estvan's partner," one eminent Froelich collector claims, "were of high quality and were widely used by the Army of Northern Virginia." For the duration of the war, North Carolina armed and supplied its 125,000 troops more effectively than any other Southern state, in large part because of the efforts of independent industrialists like Louis Froelich.[45]

Endnotes

1. William A. Albaugh III, *Confederate Edged Weapons* (New York: Harper & Brothers, 1960). See also William A. Albaugh III, *A Photographic Supplement of Confederate Swords* (Orange, Virginia: Moss Publications, 1979) (hereafter cited as Albaugh, *Confederate Swords*). Frederick R. Edmunds, "The Edged Weapons of Kenansville, North Carolina, or How to Succeed in Business by Disposing of a Rascal Partner," American Society of Arms Collectors *Bulletin* 54 (April-May 1986), pp. 11-24 (hereafter cited as Edmunds, "The Edged Weapons of Kenansville"); John T. Frawner, Jr., "Louis Froelich: Immigrant Sword Maker," American Society of Arms Collectors *Bulletin* 66 (May 1992), pp. 11-17 (hereinafter cited as Frawner, "Louis Froelich: Immigrant Sword Maker,"); John W. McAden, Jr., "A Newly Identified Kenansville Confederate Sword," American Society of Arms Collectors *Bulletin* 76 (May 1997), pp. 57-59. See also John W. McAden, Jr., "The Allure of the Froelich Staff and Field Sword," *North South Trader's Civil War Magazine* 32, no. 3 (2007), pp. 38-40. Cape Fear historian Robert J. "Bob" Cooke has extensively researched Louis Froelich and willingly shared material for this introduction. See Robert J. Cooke, "Sheathed in Mystery!" part 1 (December 2003) and part 2 (January 2004) *The Runner* (newsletter of the Cape Fear Civil War Round Table, Wilmington, North Carolina) (hereafter cited as Cooke, "Sheathed in Mystery!" *The Runner*). Frank E. Vandiver, *Ploughshares Into Swords: Josiah Gorgas and Confederate Ordnance* (Austin: University of Texas Press, 1952); Richard Goff, *Confederate Supply* (Durham, North Carolina: Duke University Press, 1969); Harold S. Wilson, *Confederate Industry: Manufacturers and Quartermasters in the Civil War* (Jackson: University Press of Mississippi, 2002).

2. Ninth Census of the United States, 1870: Duplin County, North Carolina, Kenansville Twp, p. 5; Tenth Census of the United States, 1880: Halifax County, North Carolina, p. 14. See also Leon H. Sikes, "The Swords of Kenansville: A Brief Study of Louis Froelich and the Confederate Arms Factory, Kenansville, NC," *Footnotes* (newsletter of the Duplin County Historical Society, North Carolina), 58 (November 1995), p. 5 (hereafter cited as Sikes, "The Swords of Kenansville," *Footnotes*).

3. Cooke, "Sheathed in Mystery!" *The Runner*, pt. 1 (December 2003), p. 3. Wilhemina Froelich's brother Charles F. Bissinger worked for Louis Froelich during and after the Civil War. Although Bissinger does not appear in the 1860 census, tax rolls, or the Wilmington directory, perhaps his residence in Wilmington attracted the Froelichs to the town. There was possibly another familial connection with Wilmington. North Carolina court records reveal that Fanny Froelich, a New York widow, married James T. Schonwald in 1843. A year after the couple moved to Baltimore in 1844, Schonwald relocated to Wilmington, North Carolina, to practice medicine. When Fanny arrived to join her husband shortly thereafter, she found him to be a changed man—cold, cruel, and abusive—and returned rapidly to familiar surroundings in New York. The couple eventually divorced, but a twenty-one year court battle ensued over alimony payments. See Schonwald vs. Schonwald in Hamilton Jones, ed., *North Carolina Reports* vol. 55, June Term (Raleigh: E.M. Uzzell & Co., 1903), pp. 343-344; Fanny Frolick v. James T. Schonwald in Hamilton Jones, ed., *North Carolina Reports* vol. 52, December 1859 Term to August 1860 Term (Raleigh: Mitchell Printing Co., 1920), pp. 427-429; Fanny Schonwald v. James T. Schonwald in S.F. Phillips (ed.), *North Carolina Reports* vol. 62, June Term 1866-1868 (Raleigh: Edwards & Broughton Printing Co., 1915), pp. 152-155. Perhaps Fanny Froelich Schonwald was related to Louis Freolich, prompting Louis to travel to Wilmington in 1861 to see Dr. Schonwald on Fanny's behalf.

4. Alan D. Watson, *Wilmington, North Carolina, to 1861* (Jefferson, North Carolina: McFarland and Co., 2003), p. 103; Wilmington *Daily Journal*, May 16, 1861. For additional information on Loeb & Swarzman, see T. Luther Jr. (ed.), *Kelley's Wilmington Directory, To Which is Added a Business Directory for 1860-1861* (Wilmington, North Carolina: Fulton & Price, 1860), p. 55 (hereafter cited as *Kelley's Wilmington Directory 1860-1861).*

5. Wilmington *Daily Journal*, May 16, 1861. "Messrs. Loeb & Swarzman have shown us some buttons made by them in this place. They are of brass, round topped, polished and about three-fourths of an inch in diameter. They look serviceable and would no doubt show very well on military uniforms. . . .These buttons are perfectly plain, as Messrs. L&S inform us that they have not been able to get the dies made as yet so as to impress them with the State arms." Wilmington *Daily Journal*, June 1, 1861.

6. Richard Taylor Hill and William Edward Anthony, *Confederate Longarms and Pistols* (Charlotte, North Carolina: Richard Taylor Hill and William Edward Anthony, publishers, 1978), pp. iv, 34, 88, 110 (hereafter cited as Hill and Anthony, *Confederate Longarms and Pistols*); Albaugh, *Confederate Swords*, pp. 11, 113, 137; Chris E. Fonvielle, Jr., *The Wilmington Campaign: Last Rays of Departing Hope* (Campbell, California: Savas Publishing, 1997), pp. 5-6 (hereafter cited as Fonvielle, *The Wilmington Campaign*); Dawson Carr, *Gray Phantoms of the Cape Fear: Running the Civil War Blockade* (Winston-Salem, North Carolina: John F. Blair, Publishers, 1998), pp. 10-13 (hereafter cited as Carr, *Gray Phantoms of the Cape Fear*).

7. Fonvielle, *The Wilmington Campaign* p. 17; Carr, *Gray Phantoms of the Cape Fear*, pp. 17, 22: Charles L. Webster III to Chris E. Fonvielle, Jr., June 9, 2008. Information is from Lon Webster's forthcoming book, *Entrepot: Government Imports into the Confederate States* (Roseville, Minnesota: Edinborough Press, 2008).

8. Wilmington *Daily Journal*, March 16, 1855, May 21, 1861; *Kelley's Wilmington Directory 1860-61*.

9. Hill and Anthony, *Confederate Longarms and Pistols*, p. iv.

10. John M. Murphy and Howard M. Madaus, *Confederate Rifles and Muskets: Infantry Small Arms Manufactured in the Southern Confederacy, 1861-1865* (Newport Beach, California: Graphic Publishers, 1996), pp. 104-119; 419-438; 461-486 (hereafter cited as Murphy and Madaus, *Confederate Rifles and Muskets*); Hill and Anthony, *Confederate Longarms and Pistols*, pp. 34, 88, 110; Albaugh, *Confederate Swords*, pp. 11, 113, 137.

11. Wilmington *Daily Journal*, July 16, 1861.

12. North Carolina [Raleigh] *Weekly Standard*, July 24, August 7, 1861.

13. Edmunds, "The Edged Weapons of Kenansville," p. 11. See also Frawner, "Louis Froelich: Immigrant Sword Maker," p. 11. Quote is from Wilmington *Daily Journal*, September 12, 1861; Mark A. Boatner III, *The Civil War Dictionary* (New York: David McKay Company, Inc., 1959), p. 944.

14. The precise location of the Wilmington Sword Factory is unknown, although evidence suggests that it was just north of where the Cape Fear Memorial Bridge enters Wilmington. See W.H.C. Whiting to Samuel G. French, February 3, 1863, United States War Department, *The War of the Rebellion, A Compilation of the Official Records of the Union and Confederate Armies* 128 volumes. (Washington, D.C., 1880-1901), series I, volume 18, p. 868 (hereafter cited as *Official Records, Army*). See also: Wilmington *Daily Journal*, September 23, 1861.

15. Wilmington *Daily Journal*, September 26, October 24, 1861, June 7, 1862.

16. Wilmington *Daily Journal*, September 24, 1861.

17. Wilmington *Daily Journal*, September 26, October 24, November 2, 14, 1861.

18. Wilmington *Daily Journal*, November 2, 1861.

19. Wilmington *Daily Journal*, November 9, 1861. See also Cooke, "Sheathed in Mystery!" *The Runner*, pt. 1 (December 2003), p. 3.

20. Frawner, "Louis Froelich: Immigrant, Sword Maker," p. 12; Cooke, "Sheathed in Mystery!" pt. 1 (December 2003), *The Runner*, p. 3; William George Thomas to Henry T. Clark, November 30, 1861, Henry Toole Clark, Governors Papers, North Carolina State Archives, Raleigh (hereafter cited as Clark, Governors Papers, N.C. State Archives).

21. Entries for December 13, 28, 31, 1861, January 4, 6, 13, 1862, Ordnance Department Day Book, volume 27: December 16, 1861-June 1, 1863, Adjutant General Record Group, North Carolina State Archives, Raleigh (hereafter cited as Ordnance Department Day Book, vol. 27, Adjutant General Record Group, N.C. State Archives); Wilmington *Daily Journal*, December 26, 1861.

22. Wilmington *Daily Journal*, November 9, December 2, 1861.

23. Various entries from December 20, 1861 through February 15, 1862, Ordnance Department Day Book, vol. 27, Adjutant General Record Group, N.C. State Archives; Henry T. Clark to Judah P. Benjamin, March 11, 1862, *Official Records, Army*, series IV, volume 1, p. 987; Edmunds, "The Edged Weapons of Kenansville," p. 12. Military arms collectors deem surviving examples of Froelich's earliest weapons to be of the highest quality. It therefore seems likely that Froelich discarded or recycled weapons that had been rejected by North Carolina's ordnance inspectors.

24. William George Thomas to Henry T. Clark, February 24, 1862, Clark, Governors Papers, N.C. State Archives; Richmond *Examiner*, August 10, 1863; Edmunds, "The Edged Weapons of Kenansville," p. 12; Wilmington *Daily Journal*, August 15, 1863. See also Richmond *Daily Dispatch*, August 18, 1863.

25. Wilmington *Daily Journal*, March 14,1862; various entries from March through September 1862, Ordnance Department Day Book, vol. 27, Adjutant General Record Group, N.C. State Archives; Wilmington *Daily Journal*, May 17, 1862.

26. Wilmington *Daily Journal*, June 7, 23, 1862; Cooke, "Sheathed in Mystery!" *The Runner*, pt. 1 (December 2003), p. 3.

27. Fonvielle, *The Wilmington Campaign*, pp. 19-20; Leora McEachern and Isabel Williams (eds.), "Wilmington, North Carolina and the Lower Cape Fear Area During the Civil War (1861-1865): An Excerpted Guide to Resources, 1861-1865," volume 2, part 2—1862, p. 151, Special Collections, William Randall Library, University of North Carolina Wilmington. This 13 volume typescript collection, compiled and donated by Leora McEachern and Isabel Williams, consists of letters, diaries, papers, and published materials on Wilmington and the Lower Cape Fear during the Civil War.

28. Fonvielle, *The Wilmington Campaign*, p. 19; Wilmington *Daily Journal*, September 27; General Index to Real Estate Conveyances, Grantees, 1784-1940, Registrar of Deeds Office, Kenansville, Duplin County, North Carolina; Frawner, "Louis Froelich: Immigrant Sword Maker," p. 12; Sikes, "The Swords of Kenansville," *Footnotes*, p. 6; Cooke, "Sheathed in Mystery!" *The Runner*, pt.1 (December 2003), p. 4.

29. Wilmington *Daily Journal*, October 2, 1862; Fayetteville *Observer*, October 6, 1862.

30. Wilmington *Daily Journal*, November 20, 1862; Invoice of Louis Froelich, November 26, 1862 (microfilm roll 327), Confederate Papers Relating to Citizens and Business Firms, War Department Collections of Confederate Records, Record Group 109, National Archives, Washington, D.C. (hereafter cited as Confederate Records, Record Group 109, National Archives); Frawner, "Louis Froelich: Immigrant Sword Maker," p. 13; Wilmington *Daily Journal*, December 8, 17, 1862; entries from November 26, 1862 through February 28, 1863, Ordnance Department Day Book, vol. 27, Adjutant General Record Group, N.C. State Archives.

31. Wilmington *Daily Journal*, January 10, 19, 1863.

32. Wilmington *Daily Journal*, February 21, March 12, 1863; Cooke, "Sheathed in Mystery!" *The Runner*, pt. 1 (December 2003), p. 4. and pt. 2 (January 2004), p. 3.

33. Wilmington *Daily Journal*, March 25, 1863; Abstracts of Contracts, April 29, September 16, 1863, chapter 4, volume 96, pp. 416-417, Day Book and Abstracts of Contracts, Ordnance Depot, Richmond, Virginia, 1861-1863, Records of the Ordnance Department, Confederate Records, Record Group 109, National Archives; Cooke, "Sheathed in Mystery!" *The Runner*, pt. 2 (January 2004), p. 3.

34. Wilmington *Daily Journal*, May 6, November 21, 1863.

35. Report of John G. Foster, July 7, 1863, *Official Records, Army* series I, vol. 27, pt. 2, pp. 859-860; Report of George W. Lewis, July 8, 1863, *Official Records, Army* series I, vol. 27, pt. 2, pp. 860-863; Sikes, "The Swords of Kenansville," *Footnotes*, p. 6. See also: North Carolina [Raleigh] *Weekly Standard*, July 15, 1863.

36. Wilmington *Daily Journal*, November 21, 1863; Frawner, "Louis Froelich: Immigrant Sword Maker," p. 13.

37. *Kelley's Wilmington Directory 1860-1861*, pp. 29, 94; Frawner, "Louis Froelich: Immigrant Sword Maker," p. 13; Cooke, "Sheathed in Mystery!" *The Runner*, pt. 2 (January 2004), p. 3.

38. Wilmington [Weekly] *Journal*, April 28, 1864. With the exception of this newspaper article, no other extant records place Louis Froelich in North Carolina before mid-May 1861, when he was hired by Jacob Loeb and Lewis Swarzman to direct operations at the Wilmington Button Manufactory.

39. Louis Froelich to Captain James Dinwiddie, June 7, 1864, Richmond Depot Letters Received, Richmond, Virginia, March-July 1864, Volume 94; and Captain James Dinwiddie to Louis Froelich, November 9, 1864, Richmond Ordnance Depot Letters Sent, Richmond, Virginia, September 1864-February 1865, chap. 4, vol. 91 ½, both records in Records of the Ordnance Department, Confederate Records, Record Group 109, National Archives; Frawner, "Louis Froelich: Immigrant Sword Maker," p. 13.

40. General Index to Real Estate Conveyances, Grantees, 1784-1940, Registrar of Deeds Office, Kenansville, Duplin County, North Carolina; Sikes, "The Swords of Kenansville," *Footnotes*, p. 7.

41. *First Annual Fair of the Cape Fear Agricultural Association* (Wilmington, N.C.: Englehard & Price, 1870), pp. 44-45 (hereafter cited as *First Annual Fair of the Cape Fear Agricultural Association*).

42. *First Annual Fair of the Cape Fear Agricultural Association*, pp. 20-21, 24, 47. Louis Froelich contributed three articles, "High Farming," "The Manufacture of Wine," and "Commercial Fertilizers and Their Use," to

the First Annual Fair of the Cape Fear Agricultural Association booklet in 1870. Wilmington *Morning Star,* August 11, 12, 1870; Sikes, "The Swords of Kenansville," *Footnotes*, p. 7.

43. Wilmington *Morning Star*, November 2, 1873; Cooke, "Sheathed in Mystery!" *The Runner*, pt. 2 (January 2004), p. 4. For more on the Garrett vineyards, see: *Sketches in North Carolian, USA, 1872 to 1878: Vineyard Scenes by Mortimer O. Heath* (Raleigh: N.C. Office of Archives and History, 2001); *First Annual Fair of the Cape Fear Agricultural Association,* p. 44.

44. Wilmington *Morning Star*, November 2, 1873; Sikes, "The Swords of Kenansville," *Footnotes*, p. 7; Cooke, "Sheathed in Mystery!" *The Runner*, pt. 2 (January 2004), p. 4.

45. Edmunds, "The Edged Weapons of Kenansville," p. 12.

Most of the research and information in the Introduction by Chris E. Fonvielle, Jr., was first published in his article, "Never Suffer for Machines of War:" Louis Froelich as Arms-Maker to North Carolina and the Confederacy, *North Carolina Historical Review* (Vol. LXXXIV, No. 3, July 2007) and is reprinted here by permission of the North Carolina Office of Archives and History, Historical Publications Section.

Bibliography

Manuscripts

Henry Toole Clark, Governors Papers, North Carolina State Archives, Raleigh.

McEachern, Leora and Isabel Williams (eds.), "Wilmington, North Carolina and the Lower Cape Fear Area During the Civil War (1861-1865): An Excerpted Guide to Resources, 1861-1865," 13 volumes, Randall Library, University of North Carolina Wilmington.

Official Publications

Confederate Papers Relating to Citizens and Business Firms, War Department Collections of Confederate Records, Record Group 109, National Archives, Washington, D.C.

Day Book and Abstracts of Contracts, Ordnance Depot, Richmond, Virginia, 1861-1863, Records of the Ordnance Department, Confederate Records, Record Group 109, National Archives, Washington, D.C.

Eighth Census of the United States, 1860: New Hanover County, North Carolina.

General Index to Real Estate Conveyances, Grantees, 1784-1940, Registrar of Deeds Office, Kenansville, Duplin County, North Carolina.

Jones, Hamilton (ed.), *North Carolina Reports* volume 55, June Term, Raleigh: E.M. Uzzell & Co., 1903.

Jones, Hamilton (ed.), *North Carolina Reports* volume 52, December 1859 Term to August 1860 Term, Raleigh: Mitchell Printing Co., 1920.

Ninth Census of the United States, 1870: Duplin County, North Carolina.

Ninth Census of the United States, 1870: New Hanover County, North Carolina.

Ordnance Department Day Book, volume 27, December 16, 1861-June 1, 1863, Adjutant General Record Group, North Carolina State Archives, Raleigh.

Phillips, S.F. (ed.), *North Carolina Reports* volume 62, June Term 1866-1868, Raleigh: Edwards & Broughton Printing Co., 1915.

Richmond Depot Letters Received and Richmond Ordnance Depot Letters Sent, Richmond, Virginia, September 1864-February 1865, chapter 4, volume 91 ½, Records of the Ordnance Department, Confederate Records, Record Group 109, National Archives, Washington, D.C.

Tenth Census of the United States, 1880: Duplin County, North Carolina.

Tenth Census of the United States, 1880, Halifax County, North Carolina.

United States War Department, *The War of the Rebellion, A Compilation of the Official Records of the Union and Confederate Armies* 128 volumes. (Washington, D.C., 1880-1901).

Newspapers

Fayetteville *Observer*

North Carolina [Raleigh] *Weekly Standard*

Richmond *Daily Dispatch*

Richmond *Examiner*

Wilmington *Daily Journal*

Wilmington *Morning Star*

Wilmington [Weekly] *Journal*

Published Secondary Sources

Albaugh, William A. III, *Confederate Edged Weapons*, New York: Harper & Brothers, 1960.

Albaugh, William A. III, *A Photographic Supplement of Confederate Swords*, Orange, Virginia: Moss Publications, 1979.

Albert, Alphaeus H., *Record of American Uniform and Historical Buttons*, Boyertown, Pennsylvania: Boyertown Publishing Company, 1976.

Boatner, Mark A. III, *The Civil War Dictionary*, New York: David McKay Company, Inc., 1959.

Carr, Dawson, *Gray Phantoms of the Cape Fear: Running the Civil War Blockade*, Winston-Salem, North Carolina: John F. Blair, Publishers, 1998.

Cooke, Robert J., "Sheathed in Mystery!" part 1 (December 2003) and part 2 (January 2004) *The Runner* (newsletter of the Cape Fear Civil War Round Table, Wilmington, North Carolina).

Edmunds, Frederick R., "The Edged Weapons of Kenansville, North Carolina, or How to Succeed in Business by Disposing of a Rascal Partner," American Society of Arms Collectors *Bulletin* 54 (April-May 1986).

First Annual Fair of the Cape Fear Agricultural Association, Wilmington, North Carolina: Englehard & Price, 1870.

Fonvielle, Chris E., Jr., *The Wilmington Campaign: Last Rays of Departing Hope*, Campbell, California: Savas Publishing, 1997.

Frawner, John T., Jr., "Louis Froelich: Immigrant Sword Maker," American Society of Arms Collectors *Bulletin* 66 (May 1992).

Haskett, Delmas D. and William M. Reaves (eds.), *Oakdale Cemetery Records, Wilmington, N.C., 1852-1879*, Wilmington, North Carolina: Old New Hanover Geneaological Society, 1989.

Haskett, Delmas D. and William M. Reaves (eds.), *Oakdale Cemetery Records, Wilmington, N.C., 1880-1919*, volume II, Wilmington, North Carolina: Old New Hanover Geneaological Society, 1990.

Hill, Richard Taylor and William Edward Anthony, *Confederate Longarms and Pistols*, Charlotte, North Carolina: Richard Taylor Hill and William Edward Anthony, publishers, 1978.

Luther, T., Jr. (ed.), *Kelley's Wilmington Directory, To Which is Added a Business Directory for 1860-1861*, Wilmington, North Carolina: Fulton & Price, 1860.

McAden, John W., Jr., "A Newly Identified Kenansville Confederate Sword," American Society of Arms Collectors *Bulletin* 76 (May 1997).

McAden, John W., Jr., "The Allure of the Froelich Staff and Field Sword," *North South Trader's Civil War* 32, no. 3 (2007).

Murphy, John M., and Howard M. Madaus, *Confederate Rifles and Muskets: Infantry Small Arms Manufactured in the Southern Confederacy, 1861-1865*, Newport Beach, California: Graphic Publishers, 1996.

Sikes, Leon H., "The Swords of Kenansville: A Brief Study of Louis Froelich and the Confederate Arms Factory, Kenansville, NC," *Footnotes* (newsletter of the Duplin County Historical Society, North Carolina) (November 1995).

Sketches in North Carolina, USA, 1872 to 1878: Vineyard Scenes by Mortimer O. Heath, Raleigh: North Carolina Office of Archives and History, 2001.

Tice, Warren K., *Uniform Buttons of the United States*, Gettysburg, Pennsylvania: Thomas Publications, 1997.

Watson, Alan D., *Wilmington, North Carolina, to 1861*, Jefferson, North Carolina: McFarland and Co., 2003.

Employees of Louis Froelich's Confederate States Arms Factory
Wilmington, North Carolina, September 1861 to March 1863

Alexander Adrian
George P. Bappler
James Barnes
William E. Bird
Henry M. Bremer
John Bremer
E. Brickhouse
Benjamin Bryant
C.C. Burrows
Thomas C. Capps
William E. Collison
D. Corey
E. Corey
– Corinth
Andrew Craig
Nathaniel Craig
C.C. Curtis
Jacob Dahmer
Peter Dahmer
George Dawson
T.C. Dickinson
P. Edwards
M. Frazier
M. Goldsmith
I. Gordon
Perry Greene
George Grotjohan (Grotgen)
H. Harr
James Harriss
William Harriss
J.F. Hespe
Christian Hussel
H. James
P. Jorgenson
Stuart Kelley
Jol Kuhn
William M. Lewis
William Llevelyn
Ed Locheary
E.T. Lucas
H.W. Mason
James McCormick
Kenneth McKenzie
Emery McRae
Nic Mithler
G.T. Moore
R. Morehead
Peter Murray
Joseph Myers
Issac Neal
George A. Newell
M. Newhoff
A. Peterson
James Rone
C.N. Rowlen
Englehard Schulken
J. Seilet
John Silber
J.S. Silber
A. Skipper
– Skirper
Jerry Smith
George Steinmetz
William Stith
J.T. Stotter
Hinton Suggs
Rufus Thomas
Claus Tienken
William Ulrich
Jere Washington
Scipio Watters
J.W. Webb
Heinrich Westermann
Alexander Wilson
Daniel Wilson
James Wilson

Wilmington *Daily Journal*, June 7, 1862; Eighth Census of the United States, 1860: New Hanover County, North Carolina; Ninth Census of the United States, 1870: New Hanover County, North Carolina.

CS

NOMENCLATURE

SWORD HILT

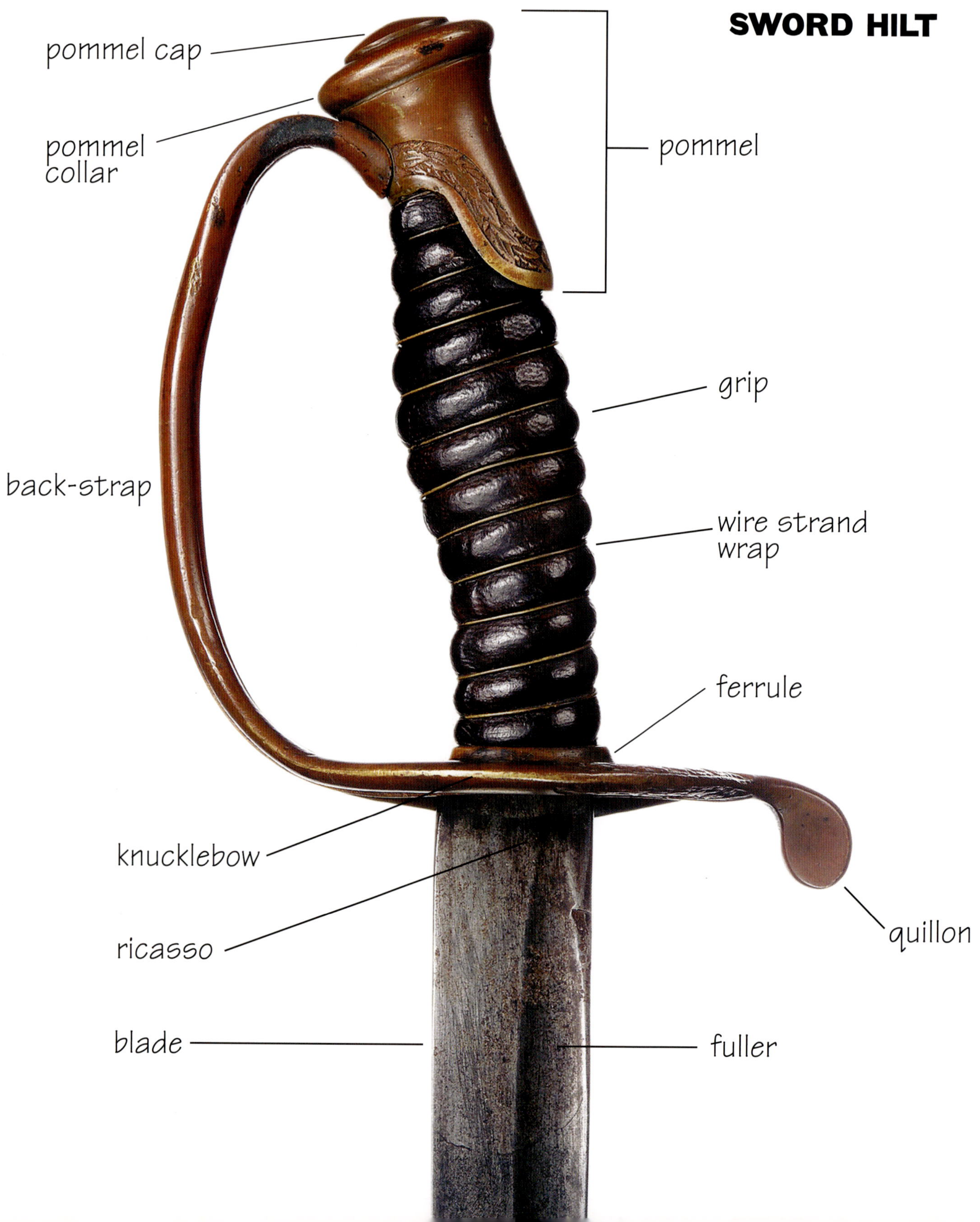

pommel cap

pommel collar

pommel

grip

back-strap

wire strand wrap

ferrule

knucklebow

ricasso

quillon

blade

fuller

SCABBARDS

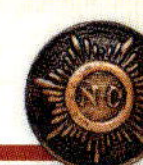

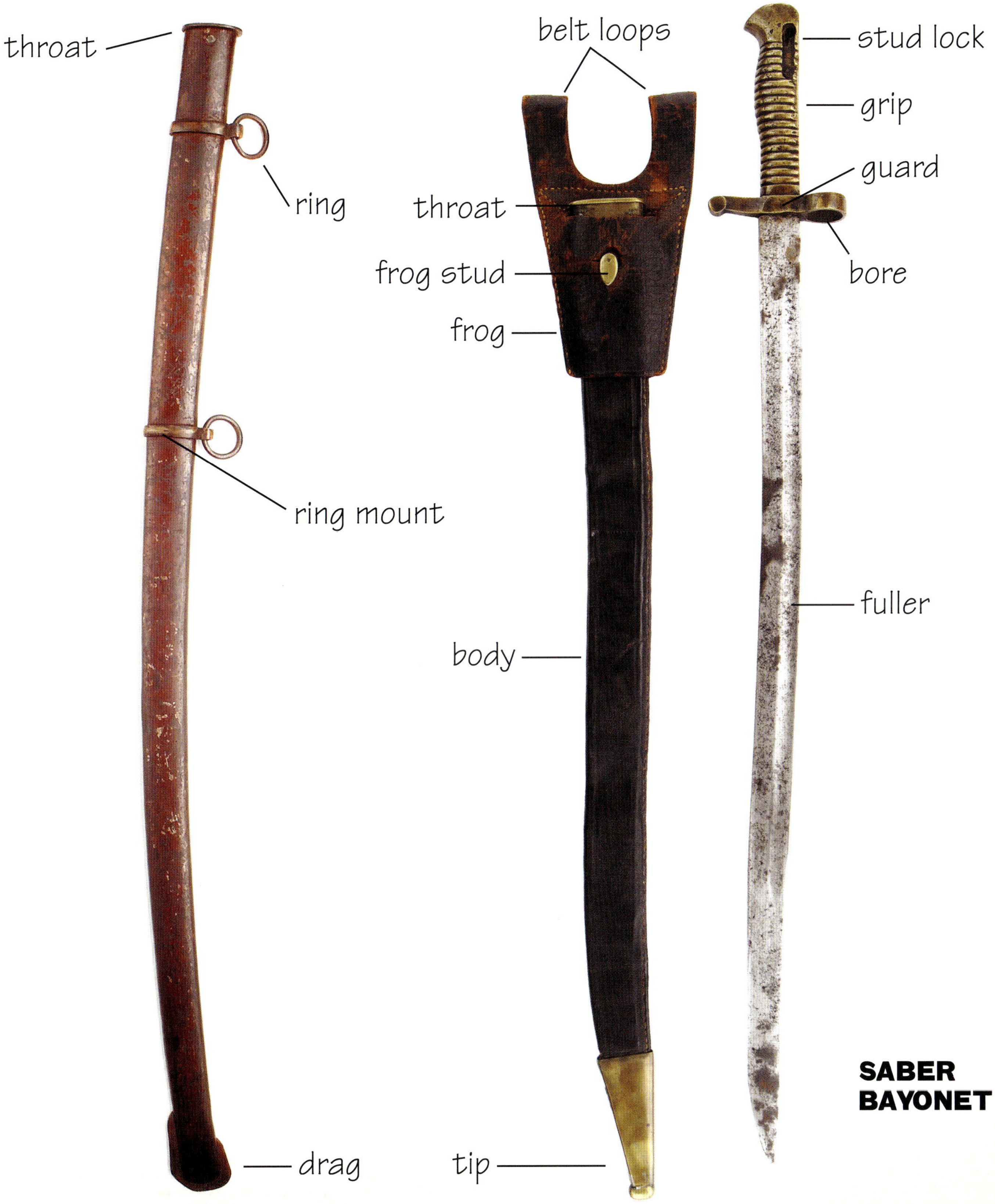
throat
ring
ring mount
drag
belt loops
throat
frog stud
frog
body
tip
stud lock
grip
guard
bore
fuller
SABER BAYONET

Staff and Field Sword

LF 1861, CS and Star

The Froelich staff and field sword with "LF 1861" on the back-strap was well designed and manufactured and most likely Froelich's earliest model sword. Because of its scarcity, it was probably made on special order.

Two types of steel blades were forged: the first was a flat 1 ¼ inches wide and 29 ½ inches long blade from the hilt to the tip, with an unstopped fuller on both sides (LF 1861.1). The second was a flat 1 inch wide and 30 inches long blade with an unstopped fuller on each side (LF 1861.2). The fuller on both blades measured 20 inches to 21 inches long.

The brass guard featured a classic wreath design surrounding the letters "CS" (Confederate States) with a star at the apex centered between two branches of the wreath. The style of the guard was similar to the guards found on Confederate staff and field swords manufactured by Boyle and Gamble of Richmond, Virginia. Most back-straps on Froelich's swords were etched "LF 1861." The wooden grip was carved with a slight swell in the center, and wrapped in dark brown leather and bound with a double strand of twisted brass wire.

LF 1861.1

LF 1861.2

Froelich's LF 1861 staff and field sword scabbards were made of leather with brass ring mounts. Of four scabbards examined, one may have been made by Boyle and Gamble, another was similar to a scabbard found with a B. Douglas staff and field sword, while the two remaining scabbards featured ornate brass mounts and drags as in figure LF 1861.2.

There are seven extant examples of this sword-type. One is a battlefield relic, while the remaining six survived the war in fine condition. One sword preserved in the collection of the Greensboro Museum in Greensboro, North Carolina, belonged to Colonel Oscar Ripley Rand of the 3rd Regiment North Carolina Home Guard. The obverse side of the blade is etched "Presented by the 3rd Regt. NCHG to Col. O.R. Rand November 7, 1864," while the reverse side of the blade is etched "L. Froelich & Co., Kenansville, N.C." (LF 1861.2).

This is the only known Froelich staff and field sword with "CS" and star cast into the hilt but without "LF 1861" on the back-strap.

CS

STAFF AND FIELD SWORD

CSA ON A RIBBON

This was a beautiful small sword with a floral design of laurel leaves in the knucklebow on the guard. A small ribbon with "CSA" (Confederate States of America) was cast in a ribbon that adorned the hilt.

The steel blades were 30 inches long and manufactured in two widths—1 inch for the standard blade (S&F.1) and 1 ¼ inches for the wide blade (S&F.2). The fuller on both sword variations was 21 ½ inches long and began ¾ inch from the hilt.

The hilt was 5 ½ inches long with the grip being wrapped in either dark brown or black leather and wound with a single strand of brass wire. As was fairly common with Froelich's swords and sabers, crude Roman numerals were usually carved into the front edge of the quillon.

The scabbards were made of iron with brass ring mounts, but rings and drags were made of either brass or iron. The scabbard's throat was sometimes marked with Roman numerals, and both swords and scabbards were sometimes lacquered red or black.

These are scarce swords with only eighteen known examples.

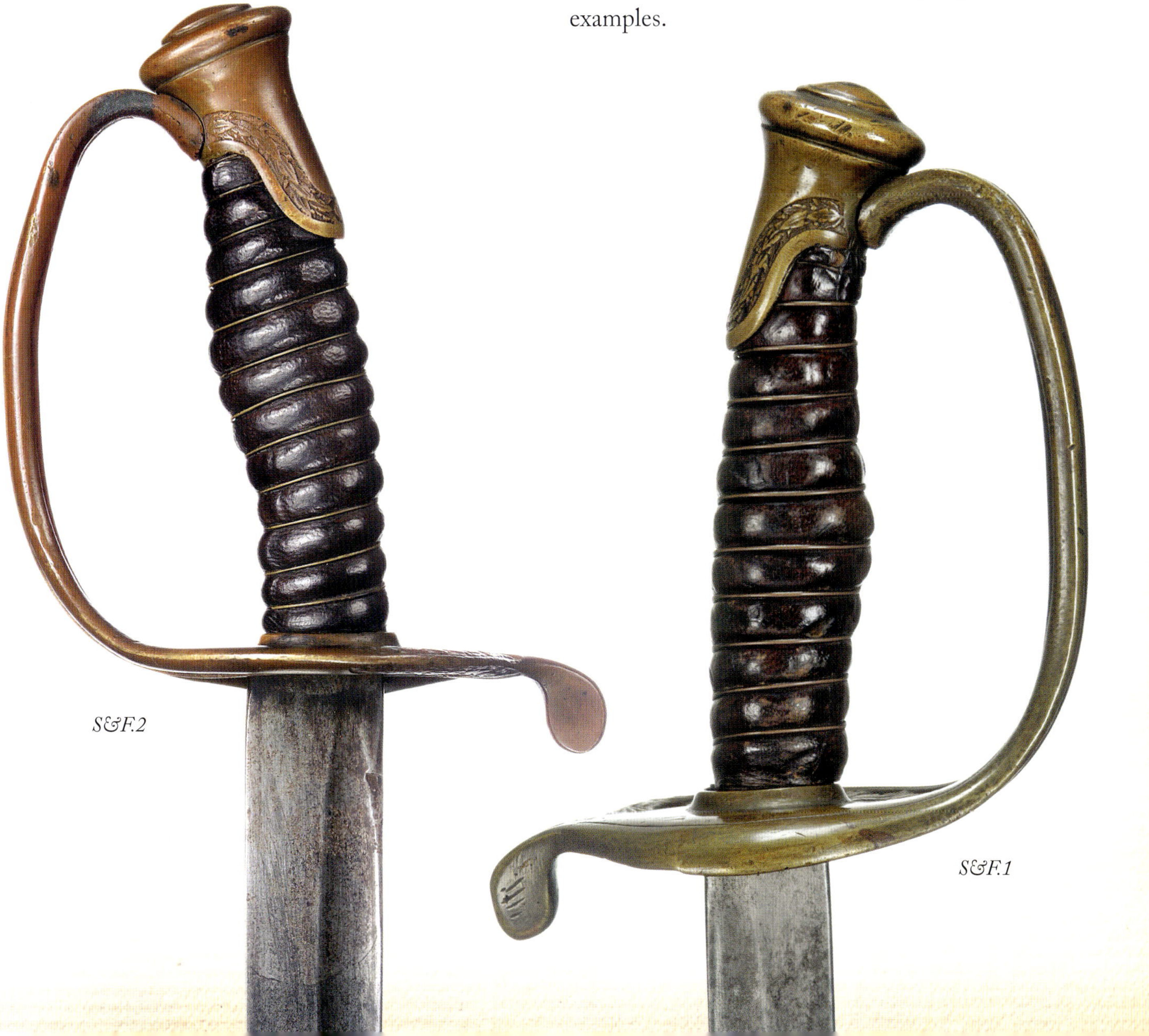

S&F.2

S&F.1

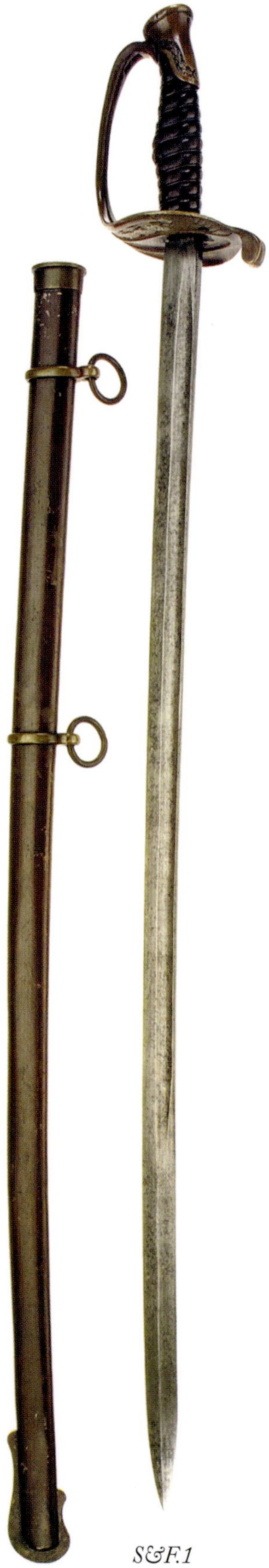

S&F.1

S&F.2

IIII
XXXVIII

Staff and Field Sword
CSA

One of the most recognizable and sought after Confederate edged weapons is Froelich's staff and field sword with CSA cast into the hilt. They were well constructed and good serviceable weapons.

The steel blades all tended to be similar in appearance, but there were actually four different types: wide, standard, narrow, and etched.

The wide blade was 30 inches long, 1 ¼ inches wide, and tapered to ¼ inch at the top of the blade. The unstopped fuller on either side of the blade began ¾ inch below the guard and measured about 29 ¼ inches to almost the end of the blade (S&F CSA.1).

The standard blade was 30 inches to 32 inches long and 1 inch wide, tapering to ¼ inch at the top of the blade. The unstopped fuller on both sides of the blade began ¾ inch below the guard and measured 21 ½ inches to 22 ½ inches down the blade (S&F CSA.2).

The narrow blade was also 30 inches to 32 inches long, 15⁄16 inch wide, and tapered to ¼ inch at the top of the blade. The unstopped fuller on either side of the blade began ¾ inch below the guard and measured 21 ½ inches to 22 ½ inches down the blade (S&F CSA.3).

The etched blade was the narrow blade with etching added. There are only four known swords with etched blades that featured two different etch patterns. Two of them were adorned with a scroll representing a vine on one side. The first pattern (not shown) featured crossed cannons 1 inch from the hilt. Below the cannons was an unfurled flag with a sunburst design in the upper corner where it joined the flagstaff. The other pattern (S&F CSA.4) also featured crossed cannons 1 inch

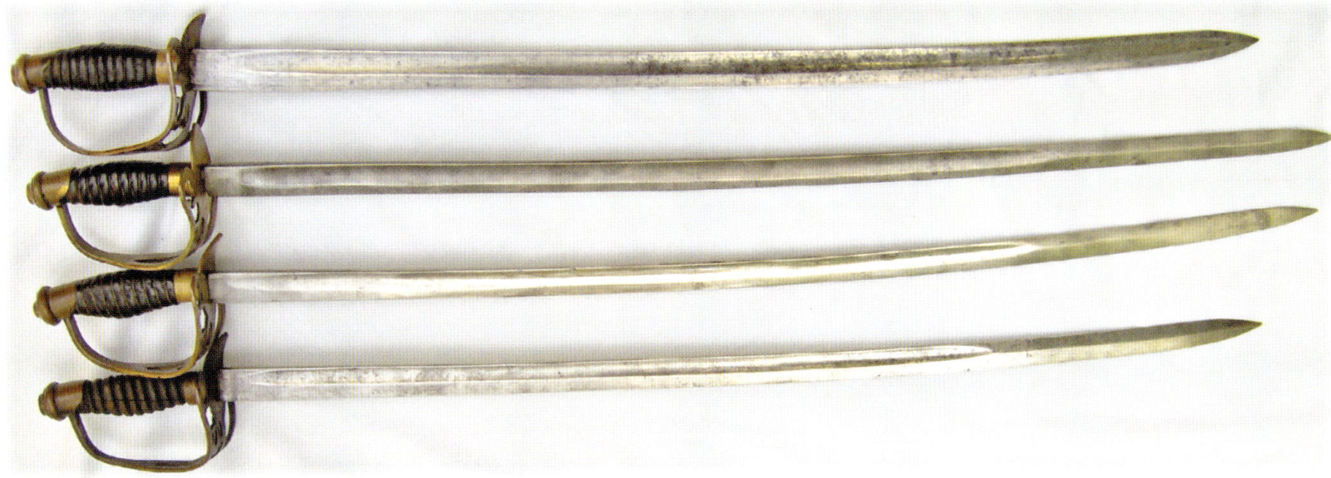

Top to bottom: S&F CSA.1, S&F CSA.2, S&F CSA.3, S&F CSA.4

Etched blade of S&F CSA.4

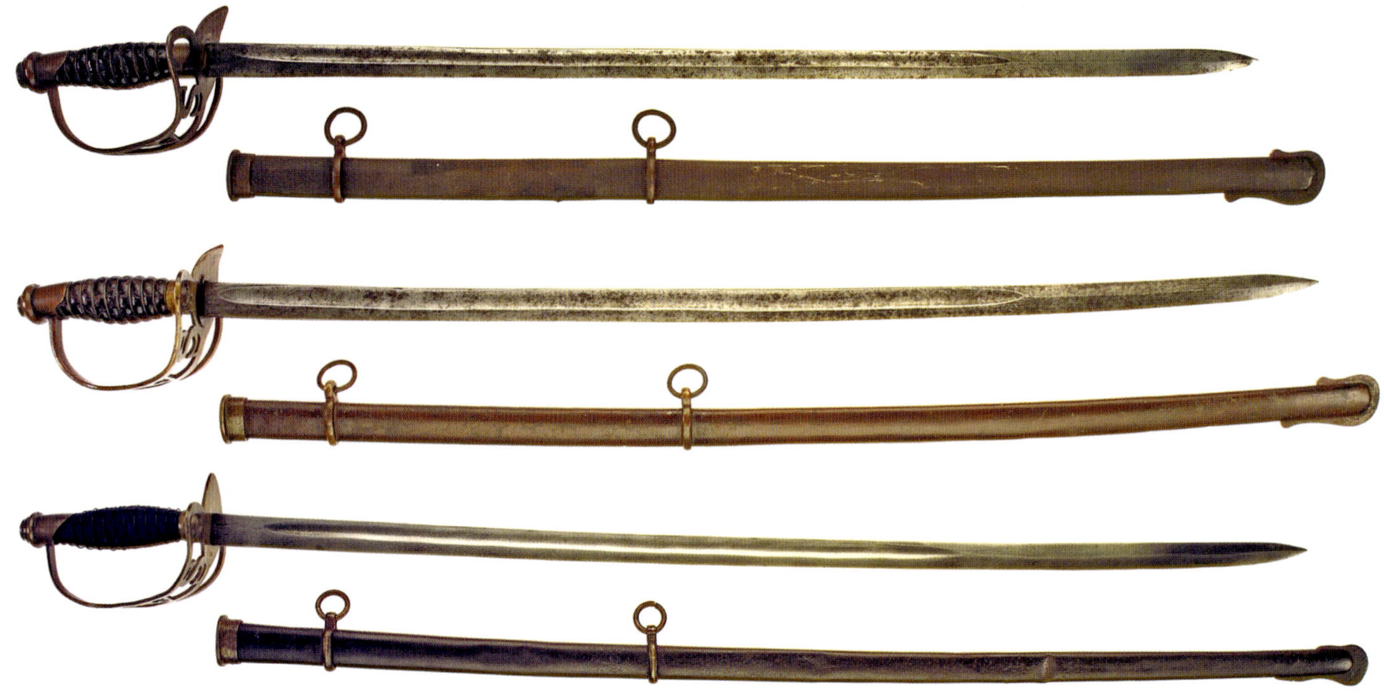

from the hilt, but below the cannons was an unfurled first national Confederate flag in the upper corner, where it joined the flagstaff.

The swords' hilts were cast of brass ranging in hue from gold to copper. Minor casting flaws were common. Roman numerals were often carved into the front edge of the quillon.

Grips on most of Froelich's staff and field swords were covered in either dark brown or black leather, but occasionally they were wrapped in oilcloth. Some leather grips were dyed white or even blue, and at least one entire sword and scabbard was lacquered red. The wraps were normally wound with 11 to 12 turns of brass or iron wire. There was usually a swell in the center of the grip. A graduated brass collar, or ferrule, ¾ inch wide encircled the grip at the base.

The brass pommels were all similar, with a rolled collar near the top which tapered up from the collar to a small flattened area on the pommel cap. The hilts generally measured 5 ⅛ inches to 5 3⁄16 inches from the top of the guard to the top of the pommel.

This Froelich staff and field sword and scabbard were lacquered red.

The CSA staff and field scabbards were made of iron with narrow brass ring mounts and rings. The iron overlapped at the seam, which was visible on the reverse or inward side of the scabbard.

The throat was made of brass and attached with two brass rivets. Three different patterns of throats are known to exist.

Drags were usually made of iron, although brass drags were not uncommon.

Officer's Cavalry Saber
CSA

To date, there are only six known examples of Froelich's officer's cavalry saber with CSA cast into the hilt.

The steel blade was 1 ¼ inches wide at the ricasso and rounded at the back. The single fuller on both sides of the blade began about ½ inch below the guard and ran 26 inches to 26 ½ inches along the blade. The total length of the blade was 34 ½ inches to 35 inches.

The guard was identical to the CSA guard found on Froelich's staff and field swords. The hilt was 5 ⅛ inches to 5 3⁄16 inches from the pommel cap to the bottom of the guard. The pommel featured a rolled collar with a flat area on the cap. The center-swelled grip was wrapped in either dark brown or black leather and wound 11 to 12 times with a single strand of iron or brass wire. A graduated brass collar or ferrule ¾ inch wide encircled the base of the grip. The hilt was sometimes marked with Roman numerals on the quillon.

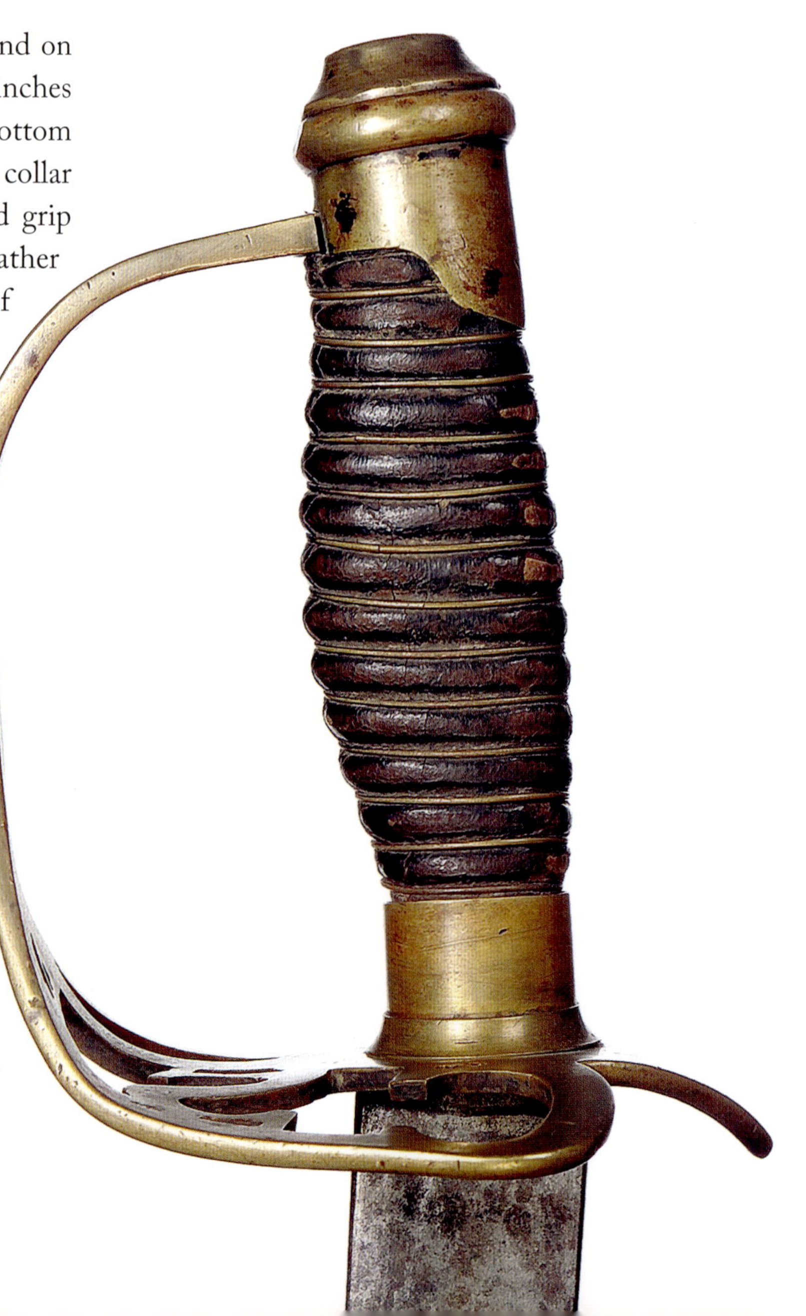

The officer's cavalry saber scabbard was made of iron and mounted with brass ring mounts and rings and either brass or iron drags. The scabbard's throat was brass and attached on both sides by brass rivets. The seams overlapped on the reverse side. Some scabbards were lacquered black or red and marked with Roman numerals. Some dealers and collectors do not believe that Froelich made cavalry saber scabbards, but purchased them from a manufacturer of generic scabbards. Similar scabbards are found with cavalry sabers of other sword-makers.

Enlisted Man's Cavalry Saber

The Froelich-made enlisted man's cavalry saber was a well made, heavy, serviceable edged weapon. It was styled after the U.S. Model 1840 cavalry saber. Evidence suggests that Froelich manufactured perhaps as many as 12,000 of these blades.

The steel blade was 1 3⁄16 inches wide at the ricasso and rounded at the back. The single fuller on both sides of the blade began about ½ inch below the guard and ran down the blade for 26 inches to 26 ½ inches. The total length of the blade was 34 ½ inches to 35 inches.

The guards were made of brass and ranged in hues from red to gold. The basket configuration of this saber differed from others in that its two branches stemmed from different points on the knucklebow, whereas the branches of other Confederate sabers stemmed from the same point on the basket. Froelich used dark brown or black leather on the sabers' grips and bound them with a single strand of brass or iron wire. Most of the sabers were marked with Roman numerals on the quillon.

The scabbards came mounted with iron rings and drags or brass rings and drags. The brass throat was attached by brass rivets on each side. The seams overlapped on the reverse side. Some scabbards were lacquered red or black and had carved Roman numerals on the top of the throat.

Short Swords

There were two distinct Froelich-manufactured short swords—an artillery model and a naval cutlass. Their manufacture was attributed to Louis Froelich by the late William A. Albaugh III and Richard D. Stewart.

The spear point blade on the artillery model measured 21 ¼ inches long and 16 inches from the "D" guard to the tip. The blade was 1⁄7 inch wide, ¼ inch thick, and had an oval shaped cross section.

The guard on the artillery short sword was cut from steel stock and measured 3⁄32 inch thick. It was ⅞ inch wide at the pommel and formed a "D" where it flared into an oval at the blade. The grip was carved from one piece of walnut through which the tang passed. The tang was peened flat on the pommel cap. The grip was basically round in shape except for a flattened area on either side running 3 ¼ inches up from the guard.

The spear point blade on the naval cutlass was 21 inches long overall, 15 ¾ inches from the guard to the point, and was oval or diamond shaped.

The guard on the naval cutlass was the same as the artillery short sword, except that the obverse side of the oval was flattened, or drawn out, to increase the size of the guard, which allowed for more hand protection as was common with most cutlasses. The one-piece walnut grip was round and contoured to fit the hand.

Scabbards for both the artillery short sword and naval cutlass were made of leather sewn together in the middle on the reverse side. The throat and lip were fashioned from tin attached with two small rivets. The belt loop was fastened to the reverse side, through the tin throat, with two piece copper rivets. The naval cutlass scabbard came reinforced with a tin tip.

There was at least one short sword variation. The "D" guard on it was cut from ⅛ inch stock and was 1 3⁄16 inches wide but did not flare into an oval, as with other Froelich short swords. It was the same width as it passed the blade to form a pointed quillon. The grip

Top to bottom: Artillery short sword, naval cutlass 1, naval cutlass 2, and short sword variation.

was made from two-pieces of walnut, fastened to a 1 1⁄16 inches wide tang and attached by three iron rivets. The thickness of the blade, guard, and tang added considerably to the weight of the short sword.

The spear point blade on this variation was 21 inches overall in length, and 16 inches in length from the guard. It measured 1 7⁄8 inches wide, 5⁄16 inch thick, and featured a diamond-shaped blade cross section.

Some artillery short sword scabbards showed a single line along both the upper and lower edges of the obverse side. Some naval cutlass scabbards were coated with waterproofing material.

The only markings on the short swords were a set of matching punch-marks found on both the tang and face of the guard. Perhaps inspection marks, they were covered by the grip. Some short swords and cutlasses were probably lacquered red as was common with other Froelich-manufactured weapons.

Reverse side of an artillery short sword scabbard with tin throat and leather belt loop.

Bowie Knives

Today the Confederate States Armory bowie knife is an extremely rare piece, with only six examples known. More knives should have survived the war. After his Union cavalry raiders burned Froelich's factory at Kenansville, North Carolina early on the morning of July 5, 1863, General John G. Foster reported to his superiors that "an armory was destroyed which contained some 2,500 sabers and large quantities of saber bayonets, *bowie knives*, and other small arms."

Froelich's bowie knives came with two guard styles. The first type featured a handle similar to that of the artillery short sword (BK.1). It was cut from stock wood 3/32 inch thick. The guard was 7/8 inch wide at the pommel and formed a "D" to the blade where it flared into an oval. The grip was one piece walnut through which the tang passed and was peened on the pommel cap. It was basically round except for a flattened area on either side running 3 ¾ inches up from the guard.

The blade was generally 1 9/16 inches wide, 15 inches long, and 3/16 inch thick, but three extant blades are 20 inches long. The blade was a typical bowie knife-type with a 4 inch clipped point.

BK.1

The second guard style was a variation of the Froelich short sword (BK.2). The "D" guard was cut from ⅛ inch stock and was 1 3⁄16 inches wide. The guard did not flare into an oval but was the same width as it passed the blade to form a pointed quillon. The grip was a solid piece of walnut roughly round in shape but with a flattened area on either side running 3 ¾ inches up from the guard, as on the first type. The blade was 1 9⁄16 inches wide, 15 inches long, and 3⁄16 inch thick with a 4 inch clipped point.

BK.2

The bowie knife sheath was made of leather folded at the seam from the bottom of the throat to the point of the clip on the top. The belt loop was 1 ⅜ inches wide and 4 ¼ inches long and sewn to the reverse side of the sheath.

One unique Confederate States Armory bowie knife featured a handle generally found on Froelich enlisted man's cavalry sabers (BK.3). The knife measured almost 15 inches overall in length. The blade itself was 9 ¾ inches long and the grip was 5 inches in length. The blade had some tooling marks but virtually no imperfections.

The guard was reshaped and expertly cut-down from its original design for a cavalry saber and fashioned into an attractive configuration for the knife. The pommel was not designed to receive a back-strap. Both the pommel and guard showed traces of original gold gilt.

The grip was wrapped in dark brown leather and wound 13 times with a single strand of iron wire. Crude Roman numeral markings were found on the left front side of the guard. The sheath is missing, but presumed to have been made of leather.

BK.3

SABER BAYONET

Froelich produced steel-bladed saber bayonets to fit rifles and muskets manufactured by mostly small, privately owned and operated North Carolina factories under state contract. Some of the noted firearm manufacturers were Asheville Armory; Clapp, Gates and Co.; Gilliam and Miller; Henry C. Lamb and Co.; Mendenhall, Jones and Gardner; Searcy and Moore; and the Florence Armory. Froelich manufactured perhaps as many as 7,000 saber bayonets during the war

The blades had unstopped fullers on both sides that ran 13 9⁄16 inches down its length. Blades varied from 19 ½ inches to 20 ¾ inches in length and 1 inch to 1 ¼ inches in width. Extant bayonets reveal many imperfections due to the various grades of iron used in the manufacture of the blades.

The saber bayonet handle was made of cast brass, but was smaller than most other brass-handled Civil War bayonets. The bore and stud guide were much the same as other period blades. The diameter of the bore on Froelich's saber bayonets came in three caliber sizes—.50, .54, and .577—as North Carolina had no standard caliber muskets and rifles early in the war. The construction of the bayonet's brass grip, however, was consistent. It was 4 ½ inches long, 1 inch thick in the middle, and the distance from the bore to the stud guide was 3 inches to 3 ¼ inches.

The saber bayonet scabbards and frogs that Froelich used, although he may have outsourced their manufacture, were made of leather. The few rare extant examples reveal that they came with either tin or brass throats 2 ½ inches long attached by two rivets on the reverse side. The scabbard tip, made of either tin or brass, was 4 inches long and held on by two rivets on the reverse side. The leather scabbard was stitched down the middle on the reverse side. The front side was decorated with lines along both the upper and lower edges. The overall length of the scabbard was 21 ¾ inches long and 1 ½ inches wide.

LANCES

Lances were made under contract for the state of North Carolina by Louis Froelich in 1861 and early 1862.

The C.S.A. Arms Factory in Wilmington manufactured two distinct types of lances. The first comprised a straight steel blade that was 18 inches long and 2 inches wide. It was secured to the shaft by a 6 13⁄16 inches long iron sleeve and a 1 inch iron pin that was braded at both ends. The lance shaft was hickory and measured 7 feet x 9 ¼ inches in length. An iron cup, 1 5⁄16 inches long, was attached to the end of the shaft by a pin ⅛ inch x ½ inch, braded only on one end (it did not go through the other side of the cup).

The second type of lance was similar to the first except for the addition of a sickle-shaped bridle cutter. The cutter was made separately from the blade and was 1 inch wide at the point, and 4 ½ inches long from the tip diagonally across to the base. Like the first model, it was secured to the hickory lance shaft with an iron pin.

According to North Carolina Ordnance Department records, 192 lances were received in Raleigh on March 26, 1862, although eight regular lances and sixteen lances with bridle cutters were rejected for being of substandard quality.

Exactly how many lances Froelich and Estvan manufactured is not known, but extant examples are quite rare. An article titled "Home Industry" in the April 28th, 1864 edition of the Wilmington [Weekly] *Journal* reported that Froelich manufactured "3,700 lance spears" during the war.

Belts & Buckles

BB.1

An Ordnance Department Day Book, Vol. 27, December 16, 1861—June 1, 1863, Adjutant General Record Group, State Archives, Raleigh, North Carolina, noted that belts and buckles were purchased from the Confederate States Armory. Froelich CSA staff and field swords and enlisted man's cavalry sabers were shipped with both belts and buckles to Raleigh.

Froelich's tongue and wreath buckle (BB.1) was smaller than the common CS version. The back of the brass tongue on Froelich's buckle had a small Roman numeral carved into it, and the reverse side of the wreath showed a distinct mold mark. The buckle retained a deep reddish color indicating a heavy concentration of copper in the brass, which was not unusual for Froelich pieces.

The belt was made of dark brown leather and was cut narrower than most Confederate belts. One extant belt originally came with sword hangers, but they were later removed. The belt was also separated from its CSA staff and field sword, ending up in the hands of one descendant, while the sword went to another.

Froelich's belt and buckle rig for both the officer's and enlisted man's cavalry sabers was patterned after a pre-war dragoon issue rig (BB.2).

According to the Ordnance Department Day Book, North Carolina purchased 877 buff leather belts and 93 officer's rigs from Froelich, although total production numbers are unknown.

BB.1

BB.1

Froelich's belt and buckle for cavalry sabers were similar to this pre-war dragoon issue belt and buckle.

BB.2

Buttons

Louis Froelich's first job in southeastern North Carolina was as director of the Wilmington Button Manufactory, which made brass ball buttons (popularly known as Zouave buttons) in the spring of 1861. Froelich's Confederate States Armory later produced military uniform buttons for North Carolina troops.

Documentation suggests that Froelich produced 800 gross (195,200 units) of military uniform buttons. Collectors and dealers generally believe that Froelich made North Carolina sunburst buttons (also referred to as starburst buttons) under state contract, identified as NC15, NC16A, NC16B and NC16C in Alphaeus H. Albert, *Record of American Uniform and Historical Buttons* and NC239 and NC242 in Warren K. Tice, *Uniform Buttons of the United States 1776-1865*. All examples were die struck copper North Carolina sunburst buttons with only minor variations to the "NC" in the circle and emanating rays on the face. The button dies probably had to be replaced after numerous strikes, thus accounting for the different patterns. The copper eyes or loops were poorly soldered to the back of the button.

NC16B

NC15

NC16A

NC16C

Miscellaneous

Louis Froelich obtained contracts to manufacture a variety of military equipment and products for both the Confederate and North Carolina quartermaster departments. Among them were cartridge boxes, percussion cap boxes, knapsacks, and haversacks–none of which have been identified to date. Froelich also made surgical instruments, vises, axes, kettles, and candles.

Swords have been mistakenly attributed to Louis Froelich because of similarities in their appearance and construction. The swords could have been made by any number of craftsmen who worked for Froelich, including George Steinmetz, who was employed as shop foreman at the Wilmington Sword Factory from September to December 1861, when he left to establish his own sword-making business in Wilmington. There may also have been some connection between Louis Froelich, B. Douglas of Columbia, South Carolina, and Boyle and Gamble of Richmond, Virginia, but no hard evidence has been found to firmly establish any association.

Some collectors believe this light cavalry saber was made by Louis Froelich because of the similarity of the Froelich-style pommel cap. The guard and grip wrapping, however, bear little resemblance to those found on Froelich's swords.

A CARD!

THE UNDERSIGNED has established a Machine Shop at Messrs. Kidder & Martin's Saw Mill, and is prepared to make Swords, Bayonetts, etc., at the shortest notice and in the most approved style. G. STEINMETZ, Formerly Foreman at the so called Confederate Arms Factory.

Dec. 21st, 1861 90-2w*

Wilmington **Daily Journal**, *December 21, 1861.*

No examples of swords and bayonets manufactured by George Steinmetz have been identified to date, although the cavalry saber below is a good candidate. Note the Roman numerals carved underneath the guard, a feature commonly found on Froelich's edged weapons and scabbards.

Light Cavalry Saber

This light cavalry saber may have been produced by Louis Froelich, although the grip, grip covering, and basket all differ from Froelich's known cavalry sabers. In fact, the guard is more similar to a Boyle and Gamble. It is possible that this unidentified "dog river" cavalry saber was made by a craftsman who had been employed at Froelich's Wilmington Sword Factory or the Confederate States Armory.

B. Douglas, Columbia, South Carolina

SWORD MANUFACTURE.

OFFICERS OF COMPANIES OR REGIMENTS NOW forming, will find specimens of my manufacture of Infantry and Cavalry Swords at the Jewelry Store of Messrs. Brown & Anderson, on Market street.

B. DOUGLAS.

June 11, 1862. 232-3t*

Wilmington Daily Journal, *June 12, 1862.*

Some military arms collectors believe that this cavalry saber was produced by Louis Froelich, referring to it as a 1st model. The only similarity to Froelich's weapon, however, was the pommel. This small sword actually more closely resembled sabers made by B. Douglas of Columbia, South Carolina, as evidenced by the grip wound with double strand brass wire, the grip's leather covering, and the back-strap.

The saber's scabbard compared favorably with Froelich's scabbards, as it did with scabbards used by other manufacturers. Perhaps one craftsman made scabbards under contract to several different arms-makers, including Froelich. More information is needed before the maker of this saber can be identified.

B. Douglas Staff and Field Sword 1

This staff and field sword resembled Louis Froelich's staff and field sword, although it was manufactured by B. Douglas. Like Froelich's staff and field swords and officer's cavalry sabers, the Douglas sword also had CSA cast into the guard. Unlike Froelich's products, however, Douglas's brass guard was more heavily cast, there was a more pronounced swell on top of the grip, and the blade was straighter. The ricasso was stamped "B. Douglas 81."

B. Douglas Staff and Field Sword 2

This staff and field sword may have been manufactured by B. Douglas, and was probably custom-made for a high ranking military officer.

The hilt featured the Froelich-style CSA but was more heavily constructed than Froelich's (note the similarity to the CSA guard of the marked B. Douglas sword on page 87). It graduated from ¼ inch at the top of the hilt to ½ inch at the guard. The guard was wrapped in kid leather with a double strand of twisted brass wire. The blade was heavy and measured 1 ¼ inches wide, 32 ⅝ inches long, and ¼ inch at the top of the blade.

Unlike all other known Froelich staff and field sword scabbards, which were made of either leather or iron, the scabbard for this sword was made of wood and lacquered black. It had both a brass drag and throat. The drag measured 5 15⁄16 inches long. The hangers were made of brass 2 ½ inches wide with small thin brass ring mounts and brass rings. The number "57" was stamped on the pommel cap. No known Froelich sword bore a similar stamping. An accompanying kid leather sleeve for the sword and scabbard had a shipping label from Adams Express Co. From Richmond, V.A.

Artillery Short Sword

Some Civil War arms' collectors and dealers believe that this scarce Roman-model short sword, of which there are several known examples, was manufactured by Froelich's Confederate States Armory. Additional information is needed, however, to confirm the supposition.

Pine Tree Button

The rare North Carolina Pine Tree button (Albert NC12, Tice NC251) may have been made at Louis Froelich's factories. Because there are so few extant examples of the button, all of which have been excavated, production of them was undoubtedly limited. The flat, one-piece constructed button was made of brass and measured 21mm in diameter. Its motif depicted a pine tree with a coiled snake around its trunk. The device was encircled by a raised ring and North Carolina and five stars on the outside of the ring.